"This book is a help not only for grieving parents but also for those called to help bear with them the burdens of such loss. And that call is for all of us."

Russell Moore, Editor-in-Chief, Christianity Today;
Author, *The Storm-Tossed Family*

"I cannot recommend this book highly enough. A wonderfully helpful, honest and practical resource for all who grieve the loss of a child, and for those who want to support them. Dan and Anna have walked this path and their writing combines authentic first-hand experience with profound spiritual and biblical wisdom. Please read this brilliant book and then pass it on to someone you know who is grieving."

John Wyatt, Emeritus Professor of Neonatal Paediatrics,
University College London; Author, *Dying Well*

'This book is so practical, thorough and encouraging. I wish I had had it when I lost my daughter to cancer several years ago, as I had to wade through so much of this alone. Dan and Anna's words are like a friend who gives it to you straight—no nonsense, yet steeped in love. This book is relevant to anyone who is grieving loss or who loves a grieving person. Read it with an open heart, and let hope wash over you."

Kate Merrick, Author, *And Still She Laughs* and *Here, Now*

"This book is a beautiful example of the sharing of Christ's comfort (2 Corinthians 1 v 3-6). We give thanks for the life of Jed, which enabled his parents to write it. It is friendly, warm, clear, deep, personal, challenging and immensely practical. Not only is it a great resource for grieving parents, it should be read by all Christians who want to be prepared to walk alongside the broken-hearted in their church family. We urge you to read it."

Elly and Dan Strange, Director, Crosslands Forum

"Navigating the waves of grief can be overwhelming, especially following the loss of a child. In this vulnerable, honest, sensitive, and biblically rich book, the Martins help fellow sufferers deal with their sorrow. They show over and over again that lamenting is good, but it is not the end. Even in the loss of a child, Jesus is near. Whether you need *Near to the Broken-Hearted* for the encouragement of your own soul, or as a resource to care for others who are dealing with grief (or for both of these reasons!), you will find it a faith-building, hope-giving read."

Tony Merida, Pastor, Imago Dei Church, Raleigh, NC;
Author, *Orphanology* and *Love Your Church*

"Those enduring the excruciating pain of child loss don't need empty promises and hurtful clichés, but words that breathe hope and comfort into their shattered world. This is what *Near to the Broken-Hearted* provides—giving space to acknowledge what's been lost and grieve what may never be, yet also to find comfort in Christ's presence and the hope of what's to come."

Sarah Walton, Author, *Hope When It Hurts* and
Together Through the Storms

"This book isn't theoretical. Every chapter—every word—is the result of walking a path of immense pain and trauma. The counsel given here isn't trite or superficial but warm, compassionate, practical and God-centered—and rich with gospel hope for those facing the worst sort of loss. It will help give voice to your lament and show you the hard questions the Holy Scriptures ask and contemplate. You will find truthful conversation partners in Dan, Anna and Chris. I highly commend *Near to the Broken-Hearted*."

Joey Tomlinson, Author, *The Day of Trouble*;
Pastor, Deer Park Fellowship, Newport News, VA

NEAR

to the

BROKEN

HEARTED

DAN & ANNA MARTIN

WITH CHRIS MOURING

thegoodbook
COMPANY

Near to the Broken-Hearted
© Dan & Anna Martin 2023

Published by:
The Good Book Company

thegoodbook.com | thegoodbook.co.uk
thegoodbook.com.au | thegoodbook.co.nz | thegoodbook.co.in

ISBN: 9781784988555 | JOB-007145 | Printed in Turkey

Cover design by Jennifer Phelps | Art Direction and design by André Parker

Contents

Foreword *by Tim Challies*   7

Introduction   9

1. Weeping with Jesus   13
   For those who've heard bad news

2. Under a Shadow   27
   For those facing future loss

3. Walking the Valley   39
   For those reeling from recent loss

4. After the Storm   53
   For those continuing to grieve

5. A Short and Precious Life   67
   *For those facing the loss of an infant or
   unborn baby*

6. Past, Present, Future *(by Chris Mouring)*   79
   For those facing the loss of an older child

7. Valuable   93
   *For those facing the possibility that their
   child will be disabled*

8. Walking Together   107
   For family and friends

9. Why Won't Jesus Heal My Child?   119

10. What Happens to Little Ones   133
   When They Die?

11. From Tears to Shouts of Joy   147
   All chapters lead here

Appendix I   159
Further practical advice for grief

Appendix II   169
Further reading and resources

Acknowledgements   173

Foreword

by Tim Challies

It was in November of 2020 that my family endured our greatest sorrow. For it was in November of 2020 that the Lord very suddenly and unexpectedly called my son Nick to himself. Nick was a student at the Southern Baptist Theological Seminary. He was newly engaged. He was looking forward to a lifetime of marriage and ministry. And then in a moment he was gone. And our hearts were broken.

But we learned very quickly that the Lord is near to the broken-hearted. We learned that he saves those who are crushed in spirit. We learned that he does not break a bruised reed and he does not quench a smouldering wick. We learned that he extends to his people all the compassion of a father to his children.

One of the ways the Lord extended his comfort to us was through his people. Particularly, through people who had endured the very sorrow we were enduring. We learned there is a sweet ministry through the written word.

Among those who reached out to us with words of comfort, compassion, and challenge was Chris Mouring, who has contributed a chapter to the book you are reading right now. And I know that if we went through our tragedy again today, this very book—the chapter he contributed as well as those written by Dan and Anna Martin—would be a source of great blessing to us.

Whether you are grieving the loss of a child, coming alongside someone who has, or simply preparing yourself to better serve others in the future, this book will be a steady and faithful guide. It will lead you to the word of God, it will assure you of the character of God, and it will comfort you with the purpose of God. It will assure you that our God is true to his every promise. He is near to the broken-hearted.

Introduction

*The LORD is near to the broken-hearted
and saves the crushed in spirit.*

Psalm 34 v 18

Grief can make you feel that you are in a storm from which you doubt you will ever emerge. You might be in the midst of a darkness so empty and bleak that you doubt it will ever clear. The heartache—the broken-heartedness—is an exhausting, crushing, daily reality. It lingers for a long time.

Maybe you have just learned some devastating news that puts the future of your child in the balance. Maybe you have lost a little one through miscarriage or stillbirth. Maybe you have had the joy of knowing and holding your child—but it has given way, far too soon, to the desperate grief of loss. Maybe the storm has long since passed according to the calendar, but the grey clouds remain. You feel broken-hearted and crushed in spirit. This is a book for you.

Or maybe you are not a parent in this situation, but a grandparent, a brother or sister, a friend, or a member of their church family. The ripples of these kinds of grief are deep and wide. This is a book for you, too.

If you doubt that comfort will ever be possible, that's ok.

Part of what it means to be "crushed in spirit" is that you struggle for hope itself. But hope doesn't rest on your ability to perceive it; hope rests with the living God. "The LORD is near to the broken-hearted and saves the crushed in spirit." God has the ability to comfort those who have lost all capacity for comfort; he has a special, tender nearness for people like you.

People like *us*. We had a baby son, Jed, who died after living for three weeks. We learned the news at our 12-week pregnancy scan that he had very significant health issues, likely to result in his death. We know what it is to have prayed, pleaded, and fasted for God to heal, and for those prayers not to have been answered. Chris, who writes in chapter 6, knows these things too: he lost his 20-year-old son, Brian, in a sudden tragic accident. Throughout the book, the three of us will share some parts of our own stories in the hope that they will offer some comfort, connection and practical help to you.

But this book is not primarily about our stories. And we are not claiming to know everything there is to know about grief. Nor are we setting out to give in-depth intellectual answers to questions about suffering. There *is* practical help for grief here, and there *are* answers to serious questions, but our main aim is to point you to the Lord Jesus. We are claiming that his grace will be enough to sustain you. We want to show you the nearness of God, in Jesus, to the broken-hearted.

You don't necessarily need to consider yourself a follower of Jesus to read this book. But we are writing this as people who have known, loved and followed Jesus for many years. And so we write to commend his tender mercies to you, whatever your journey and story.

In the famous children's book *We're Going on a Bear Hunt* by Michael Rosen and Helen Oxenbury, a group of children go out to hunt a bear. They have to pass through various obstacles—like rivers, mud and snowstorms—along the way. At each obstacle they repeat the line:

We can't go over it. We can't go under it. Oh no! We've got to go through it!

How on earth do you prepare for a pregnancy you had never thought you would have; one which will likely end in death? How do you navigate parenting a severely ill child? How do you cope with the daily acknowledgment that the one you loved has gone? Much as we would wish to go over or around this obstacle, there is no alternative: we have to go *through* it.

But we do not go alone. Jesus, the great and gracious Shepherd, is the one who carries his people *through*.

This book has eleven chapters, and not every reader will read all of them! They focus on different situations, moments, questions and experiences. Choose the ones that will be the most helpful to you; read slowly if you need to, giving yourself space to return to other chapters weeks or even months later. But please do at some point consider the final chapter. There, we reflect on the life to come—life beyond death—brought about by Jesus' resurrection. It is this which underpins and makes sense of all the other chapters.

We have written this book because there is something worth writing about, and it is this: there is comfort for the broken-hearted because Jesus died and rose. He calls out:

Behold, I am making all things new!

(Revelation 21 v 5)

1. Weeping with Jesus

For those who've heard bad news

Have you noticed how bad news has a way of reorganising your life in an instant? It carves a home for itself in the centre of your heart and moves in without your permission. Grievous news about a person you love is a plague of locusts which chews at everything, removing the life you knew.

We will never forget the day we learned the news about our son Jed's health problems. It was New Year's Eve 2018. We were attending our 12-week pregnancy scan when we found out. A few weeks prior, an early pregnancy scan had shown us the surprising and delightful image of two heartbeats. Our daughters, Lois (then aged four) and Esther (aged two), were overjoyed at the prospect of not one but two babies joining the family, so we brought them along to the second scan, expecting it to be an all-round joyous occasion of seeing twins on the screen.

It was a freezing cold, dark evening and we'd had to park quite far from the hospital as there were no spaces nearby. Dan sat both girls on his lap while Anna got started with the sonographer. From the moment the scan started we knew there was a serious problem. The sonographer stopped talking altogether, as did her trainee. And on the screen we could see a large black space in the middle of one of the babies' bodies; a problem we would soon learn was called *megacystis*—a huge bladder filled with urine. The urine was slowly accumulating as there was no way for it to drain out; a tiny outlet valve hadn't developed properly in Jed's body. Over the coming months, the pressure from his huge bladder would damage his kidneys and prevent his lungs from developing normally.

The staff said it would be easier to explain what they were seeing without the children in the room. I (Dan) hastily picked up our two girls and took them out. We walked back to the car through the freezing cold. I was barely able to say anything to my daughters, who were full of questions and worry.

We learned that evening that megacystis was *bad news*. The problems it would create for Jed's lung development meant that he would likely die shortly after birth. I called both our parents to let them know the terrible news. My mother-in-law later told us that she thought to herself that day, "We'll never laugh again".

Perhaps you feel like that too. You, or someone you love, have received some devastating news. You know that your life will never be the same again now—it can't be. As you reel, we want to invite you throughout this chapter to notice just one thing: when terrible tidings crash into our lives, *the Lord Jesus is present to weep with us*. Where others may be silent, distant, flippant, superficial and clumsy, Jesus is present, sure-footed, tender and true. The God of the Bible weeps *with us* at bad news.

THE TRUE LIE OF THE LAND

One thing which surprised us as the bad news sank in was how uncomfortable some people were with the sadness of our situation—as if they were unable to allow it to occupy a part of their world. One person responded to the news of Jed's medical problems with "Oh, you have to think positive, and it will be fine." Maybe you have had a similar experience. Such an insistence on flippant speech and superficial positivity can be crushing for those who are hurting. The same problem is revealed when people ask if you're feeling "back to normal" or if you've "got over" your grief. If you're like us, you want to cry out, "There never will be that old normal again!" Truly bad news is not like a pebble dropping into a still pond, which after a while returns to its stillness. Truly bad news is not an inconvenience which we have to wait out. Truly bad news reorganises everything, in a way we can't control. It's why we talk of being *devastated*. It's why we never move on from grief, but move on *with* grief, thankfully in changing forms.

In contrast, one of the most comforting things someone said to us during that time was simply, "Oh, I am devastated for you." He said it like a knee-jerk reaction—immediately, sincerely, and without deep thought. He honestly communicated his reflex, honest feeling. He didn't try to pretend to live in a dream world or try to pull us into a deceptive trance of positivity. He was prepared to feel sad for us and sad with us, because we should feel sad about sad things.

Your trial—and our trial—begins with bad news. And part of the trial is the simple fact that our culture doesn't know what to do with bad news. But the Bible most certainly does.

Have you ever had to walk a journey you'd normally drive? When you walk, you notice aspects of the journey which you'd previously always sped past and missed. Now, walking, you have no choice but to hear, see, and smell *the true lie of the land*. In the same way, suffering invites us into the true lie of the land of Scripture. In the Bible's pages we see a God who knows suffering. A God who comforts those who suffer. A God who gives us words of lament to help us express our grief and loss. We see a God who ultimately suffers in our place to remove suffering altogether. In the past we may have sped past these things, but now we're forced to stop and look.

We tend to distort Bible figures into superhumans, assuming that they didn't feel the same kind of pain we feel. But when we do that, we miss out on the comfort of knowing that many of them too were devastated by bad news—and were held by God through it all. Think of Naomi, who asked people to call her "Mara", meaning "bitter", because of the bitterness of losing her husband and two sons (Ruth 1 v 20). Think of David when his family had been kidnapped, and his army, having lost their families too, talked of stoning him (1 Samuel 30 v 1-6). Think of Stephen's death, and the godly men who buried him and "made great lamentation over him" (Acts 8 v 2).

And think of Jesus, weeping as he entered Jerusalem (Luke 19 v 41-44), and Jesus "greatly distressed and troubled" the night before his crucifixion (Mark 14 v 33). Jesus is prepared to be very sad about very sad things. He is the Lord who comes *especially* near to the broken-hearted and knows *especially* the pain of sad things.

The God of the Bible knows all about bad news. He is not taken by surprise. He does not stand far off and aloof when we are devastated by it.

WEEPING WITH JESUS

The story of Jesus and his friend Lazarus, found in the Bible in John 11, became one of many precious passages for us. The story begins with Jesus hearing that his friend Lazarus is dying. One reason the story is so famous is that Jesus says those wonderful words, "I am the resurrection and the life" (John 11 v 25), and then proves this by raising Lazarus back to life. But here let's focus on another reason the story is famous: Jesus arrives at his friend's tomb, and weeps.

> *Now when Mary [one of Lazarus' sisters] came to where Jesus was and saw him, she fell at his feet, saying to him, "Lord, if you had been here, my brother would not have died." When Jesus saw her weeping, and the Jews who had come with her also weeping, he was deeply moved in his spirit and greatly troubled. And he said, "Where have you laid him?" They said to him, "Lord, come and see." Jesus wept. So the Jews said, "See how he loved him!" (John 11 v 32-36)*

Jesus went. Jesus wept. Jesus was "deeply moved" in spirit. That last phrase, "deeply moved", is worth us pausing on. A more literal translation would be, "He was outraged in spirit" (see D.A. Carson, *The Gospel According to John*, p 415). Originally coming from a verb referring to the snorting of horses, this word has the sense of profound indignation and outrage. Jesus feels this "in his spirit", in himself: his inner reaction to this tomb, and the grief that surrounds it, is to be outraged and troubled.

What is he troubled and angered about? At the complete package of brokenness that this situation represents. His friend, dead and buried. People weeping all around.

Death had no part in God's original design for the world. There was no painful severing of relationships at the beginning. Yet sin entered, and so death and mourning. This is what Jesus came to confront. This is what he came to give his life in order to put right.

And Jesus felt this anger and wept those tears *even though* he was about to raise Lazarus. Even the certainty of death defeated does not remove the sadness and the outrage of bad news in the here and now. We have permission to feel and not to deny the anger which floods in. We *should* snort and bellow with anger at times. Our heartache is not failure. Children should not die!

DON'T BE AFRAID

There *are* some parts of the Bible, however, that can make us feel like we shouldn't be weeping. Have you ever read passages like these and thought, are these people really human?

Psalm 112 speaks of what someone's life is like when they are right with God:

> *He is not afraid of bad news;*
> *his heart is firm, trusting in the LORD. (Psalm 112 v 7)*

Proverbs 31 celebrates the life of a godly woman:

> *Strength and dignity are her clothing,*
> *and she laughs at the time to come.*
> *(Proverbs 31 v 25)*

When Job hears of the sudden loss of all his wealth and the deaths of all his children, he says:

> *The LORD gave, and the LORD has taken away; blessed be*
> *the name of the LORD. (Job 1 v 21)*

And then there's Sarah, Abraham's wife, of whom it is written:

And you are her children, if you do good and do not fear
anything that is frightening. (1 Peter 3 v 6)

Reading passages like these, you might find yourself wondering, *how?* How can I not fear bad news, or things that are actually frightening? How can I "laugh at the time to come" when I don't know what it'll hold? How can I bless the name of the Lord when I've lost so much? Am I really supposed to take this seriously?

After Jed died, we had a small service with family and close friends in the cemetery as we buried Jed's body. Later that same day we had a larger thanksgiving service in our church building, to thank God together for his life. We both said a few words at this thanksgiving service. One of the things we shared from the front was that same quotation from Job: "The LORD gave and the LORD has taken away; blessed be the name of the LORD". And honestly, we meant it. We still mean it.

We're not saying it was easy. On that cold December night, after the scan diagnosing Jed's megacystis, Anna made her way to an empty hospital bathroom and howled. She cried in a way she has never done before or since. But our crying was to the Lord. We grappled and struggled repeatedly through the pregnancy. We still struggle with the ongoing reality of our loss. But please hear us say this with gentle, tearful, weather-beaten sincerity: what the Bible says about walking through bad news is completely true. There is another side to what you are going through. It really is possible for the Lord Jesus to lead you through this dark valley, guarding your mind and heart in such a way that you are able to bless him in the face of bad news.

Devastating news makes us think, "We'll never laugh again". But we did. We have laughed many times since. How? Let's think a little more about those passages.

A DIFFERENT KIND OF FEAR

In Proverbs 31, the wise woman "laughs" at the days to come. How come she doesn't hold a knot of deep anxiety and unease about the days to come? On the surface of things, you might think it's because she's so energetic and organised. She's a superwoman with everything together. But the key to the whole chapter is that she's a "woman who *fears* the LORD" (Proverbs 31 v 30). Similarly, Psalm 112 is talking about a man who "*fears* the LORD" (Psalm 112 v 1). And the opening description of Job tells us that he "*feared* God" (Job 1 v 1).

It seems like "fearing the Lord" is something that can help us face bad news with courage. So we need to ask, what does "fearing the Lord" really mean?

In the Bible, fearing the Lord means *relating to God as he really is*. People who truly know God fear him. But to fear him is not to cringe in terror from him. Rather, fearing him is a parallel to loving him (see Deuteronomy 6 v 2, 5; 10 v 12; for more on this topic, read Michael Reeves' excellent book *Rejoice and Tremble*). Fearing the Lord means loving him with a love which fits the fact that he is the living God.

When the prophet Isaiah wrote about Jesus Christ hundreds of years before his birth, he said that "His delight shall be in the fear of the LORD" (Isaiah 11 v 3). And through Jesus we are invited into the same *delight* of fearing the Lord. When we see God's love and glory revealed in Jesus, especially in his death and resurrection, we too want to draw near in trembling love.

Fearing the Lord does *not* mean that we'll never hear bad news. It does not mean we'll never feel sad, devastated or achingly numb. As we've already considered, there are many examples of people in the Bible responding to bad and sad news with much weeping. Job too responds to his terrible news with great grief (Job 1 v 20). We've seen that Jesus himself is ready to enter into our grief and weep with us. But *to fear the Lord means that we don't fear other things in quite the same way.* The Lord Jesus does not call us to a life where we don't feel sadness: he invites us to a kind of life where we don't need to *fear* it.

Fearful situations are fearful because they expose our human vulnerability. They expose our lack of knowledge and our lack of control. To be told at a scan that your baby has major problems and will likely die is to come face to face with the chilling fact that you do not know what is going on, and nor can you fix it. Even to have a diagnosis doesn't provide you with the knowledge to answer questions like "Why has this happened?" and "What is my whole life going to look like now?"

The point is this: if we know—and *fear*—the living God through Jesus Christ, we need not fear what we do not know and cannot control, because we know the one who knows all and rules all for our good. The Lord Jesus does not call us to a life where we never receive bad news. Or to a life where we do not feel sad about bad news. But our Lord Jesus does invite us to live the kind of life where we do not need to fear it.

NEAR TO THE BROKEN-HEARTED

You have received bad news. Grievous news. Devastating news. A miscarriage. A stillbirth. A baby with disabilities that may cause it to die in the womb or shortly after birth. A diagnosis for your child that is not going to go away. A terrible accident.

We're so very sorry.

But we also want you to know that you have received a gracious invitation to join with other suffering people in seeing the true lie of the land; to see and to know God as he really is in the Lord Jesus, and to trust him. Your invitation is to turn to him. To weep your tears to him. To pour out your heart to him. And in so doing, to discover the comfort and intimacy of the Lord who snorts inwardly with anger at the appalling brokenness of death, the Lord who weeps with those who weep, and the Lord who is tender to the fragile and wounded.

In the coming months there may be awful things to face. It will be hard; there will be many tears. But you need not fear, since the Lord Jesus will walk with you through these dark valleys.

PRACTICAL POSTSCRIPT: METABOLISING GRIEF

Isaiah wrote:

> *You keep him in perfect peace*
> *whose mind is stayed on you,*
> *because he trusts in you. (Isaiah 26 v 3)*

Staying our minds on the Lord when we are suffering requires effort. Anxious thoughts continue to bubble up inside. But there is the possibility of peace. In this final section we want to share some practical thoughts on what it looks like to process grief with the Lord—to weep with him, to know him, and so to grow in courage.

We have found the metaphor of *metabolism* immensely helpful for talking about processing grief. Our bodies are constantly running metabolic processes which run in the background, beneath our awareness; in these processes, one thing (e.g. glucose) is turned into another thing (e.g. energy), along a "pathway". This happens in real time, doesn't stop, and varies in intensity according to what we're doing.

In the same way, grief has to be metabolised. We have to process it in real time, with no option to hit pause on the rest of life. And just like a metabolic process in the body, we have to change one thing into another: gradually, slowly, the deepest grief becomes acceptance, hope, comfort and courage. This might feel impossible to you right now, but you can do it—because the Lord has provided you with the "pathway" you need.

You may have noticed how many verses in the Bible are given over to people *lamenting*. These passages give us words to use and grooves to follow. They enable us to guide our thoughts and thus our feelings along a gospel pathway.

Take Psalm 13 as an example. It was clearly written in a place of great suffering and unanswered questioning:

> *How long, O LORD? Will you forget me for ever?*
>   *How long will you hide your face from me?*
> *How long must I take counsel in my soul*
>   *and have sorrow in my heart all the day?*
>
> (Psalm 13 v 1-2)

This is a good place to start. We can articulate our grief and fears to the Lord—crying out in outrage and distress just as Jesus did.

But the psalm doesn't stay there. In verse 5, a gospel thought is introduced:

> ***But*** *I have trusted in your steadfast love;*
>   *my heart shall rejoice in your salvation.*
> *I will sing to the LORD,*
>   *because he has dealt bountifully with me. (v 5-6)*

Do you see? The very simplest way to metabolise our squirming inner world of grief lies with one tiny word: "but". Controlling our thoughts is hard. But we can *introduce* thoughts. And that is why "but" is such a mighty word. It acts like a tiny lever that can change the whole direction and feel of a line of thought.

Let's get really practical:

1. *Simply notice what you are feeling right now. What thoughts or feelings are swirling around in your head and heart? Try to put it into some words.*
2. *Say "but".*
3. *Introduce some gospel truth; in other words, remind yourself of something true about Jesus.*

For example:

1. *I am utterly empty and numb. I can't see that I will ever come out of this.*
2. *But…*
3. *Jesus is near to the crushed in spirit.*

The sequence of what comes before and after the "but" really matters. The second statement trumps the first; it has the last word. If we inverted the above example we'd get a totally different result:

Jesus is near to the crushed in spirit, but I can't see that I will ever come out of this.

Used the right way round, "but" serves as a faithful friend to those metabolising their grief while looking at Jesus. This was us on that first night:

1. *We are devastated. We have no idea what the future holds.*
2. *But…*
3. *Nothing can separate us from God's steadfast love shown in Jesus.*

This was us repeatedly through the pregnancy:

1. *We are perplexed and both physically and emotionally exhausted*
2. *But…*
3. *The Lord's steadfast love never comes to an end.*

This is us very often nowadays:

1. *We miss Jed terribly and long to have him in our arms right now. We ache.*

2. *But...*

3. *Jesus will wipe away every tear from our eyes. We can already see beautiful things God has brought out of the bitterness for us and our children. His mercies have been new every morning. He won't leave us or ever forsake us.*

Do you see how the word "but" enables us to start metabolising our grief? It allows us to introduce a more true thought, and from there help us along a pathway towards an eventual landing place—a place of acceptance, hope, comfort and courage.

This is not easy. We will have to do it again and again, daily, hourly, every five minutes maybe; like the cells in a runner's body repeating the process of energy generation and clearance of lactate. But we can do it, because the Lord is our help.

The Lord Jesus, the Shepherd who is near to the broken-hearted, experienced terrible emotional and spiritual darkness. He gave his life—why? So that darkness and death would *not* be the final landing place for his people, but life and laughter would be instead. The life, death and resurrection of Jesus teach us what God is really like and enable us to metabolise our grief.

2. Under a Shadow

For those facing future loss

What does the word "awkward" make you think of? Perhaps a situation where someone said something *awkward*. Perhaps you've had great difficulty moving an item of furniture, not because it was heavy but because it was *awkward*. If you have an injury or a disability, some movements are *awkward*. Awkward is basically the opposite of easy and fluent.

Things become awkward as soon as it becomes clear that certain assumptions about a situation are wrong. For instance, someone might assume that congratulations are in order when they see a mother's pregnant bump. Or that a laughing child is just like any other. But what about pregnancies which unfold under an ever-darkening cloud, where each passing day seems to bring you closer to the baby's death? What about when your child is not like other children, but desperately ill? Now the interaction has gone from easy to awkward. And awkwardness is the unhappy housemate of dread, fear and desperation.

Perhaps you know these emotions; you have reason to expect that something awful is coming, and you are waiting with dread. Perhaps you have learned, as we did, that your child is unlikely to survive the pregnancy, or very far beyond. Perhaps you have recently learned that you have had a late miscarriage but have yet to face the delivery. Perhaps a scan or test has diagnosed significant health problems for your child, and the severity isn't yet clear. Perhaps you've received the devastating news that your beloved teenager is unlikely to recover from their illness.

This chapter is for all those who are anticipating something horrible. You have a whole kaleidoscope of fears and pressures, some of which are different from the ones we experienced; we humbly recognise our inability to offer counsel precisely tailored to what you are going through. Nevertheless, we believe we have help to offer—or rather, the Lord does. In this chapter we focus on learning how to navigate the awkwardness and fear that suddenly seem to surround you when loss looms: awkwardness in relating to God, awkwardness in our own emotions, and awkwardness with people.

OUT OF CONTROL

We were told that it was extremely likely that our son Jed would die shortly after birth. As the pregnancy continued, his death looked ever more likely, as the scans showed the situation getting worse. Jed's body was growing, but so was the size of his bladder—damaging his kidneys and preventing his lungs from growing.

We were in a season of prolonged out-of-control-ness. Every fortnight we would go for another scan to see how Jed was developing. We would pray and fast for healing. And each time the picture was worse. Both of us are fairly organised people who find lack of control disturbing, threatening.

We had ongoing unanswered prayers and questions: What is your plan here, Father? Why will you not heal Jed? Isn't there something we can *do* to fix all this? We were coming face to face with the awkward and uncomfortable truth that we do not control our world.

Here is a verse we kept returning to (and still do):

> *Count it all joy, my brothers, when you meet trials of*
> *various kinds... (James 1 v 2)*

This verse is decidedly awkward. It jars us. It challenges our whole world to the point of almost making us want to vomit. Consider our trials to be "all joy"?! There isn't something lost in translation here: it is the genuine opening to a letter to suffering Christians in the Bible. It's the kind of verse you might have read without much thought before, but now you cannot remain neutral: you have to decide if you are going to get furious with God for daring to say this—or if you are going to embrace this other way of navigating suffering.

> *Count it all joy, my brothers, when you meet trials of*
> *various kinds, for you know that the testing of your faith*
> *produces steadfastness. And let steadfastness have its full*
> *effect, that you may be perfect and complete, lacking in*
> *nothing. (v 2-4)*

Suffering is an invitation into a way of life where we are not the centre of gravity, but God is—where "steadfastness" (or "patient endurance") is the hallmark. We naturally panic at our lack of control. God invites us instead to prize the testing (or proving) of our faith—the growing of our trust in him, even and especially when we don't know what's going to happen.

This isn't the only thing the Bible says about suffering; in chapter 1 we saw that God weeps with those who weep, that sad things really are sad, and that desperate grief is a right response to terrible news. In later chapters we will think about how to make sense of unanswered prayer (chapter 9) and what the Bible's ultimate answer to suffering is (chapter 11). But for now, please see that the fact that God uses suffering in our lives does not mean that it is not hard or that he does not care. In fact, it is the *evidence* of his care for us. The Bible says that God has prepared "good works" for each of us to inhabit and walk in (Ephesians 2 v 8-10). God has prepared these good works like a master artisan-craftsman; nothing is mass-produced. So the specific "good works" in your life are evidence of God's tailored, targeted care for you. And persevering through trials is very much a good work. It is something that the Lord Jesus particularly prizes and treasures (1 Peter 1 v 6-7).

2 Timothy 3 v 15-17 tells us that it is Jesus' words, breathed out by his Spirit as the Bible, that equip us for every good work, including persevering. This means that outrageous commands like the one in James 1 are actually the Lord Jesus' *equipment* for us for this hard journey. They invite us to be more fully moulded by the Master Craftsman himself; to allow ourselves to be weaned off dependence on ourselves and learn dependence on him. This process is awkward; it is not easy. But it is good.

You are facing something awful; something that is emblematic of the brokenness of the world we live in; something that you would never, ever choose for yourself. But perhaps you can also begin to receive this season as God's proving of your precious faith. It is his beautiful work of growing you in steadfastness as you learn greater dependence on him.

IN BETWEEN

A liminal space is where two domains meet. It's an in-between space. You are on the verge of something, but it hasn't happened yet; you don't know exactly what to expect. The experience of being in a liminal space is unsettling and difficult. It's awkward.

After Jed's diagnosis, we were in a liminal space; our child was alive yet was somehow close to death. During pregnancy, Anna used to find driving past our local cemetery hard, knowing that Jed who was then safe and warm inside her would soon be cold and buried. The dissonance was unbearable.

This liminal experience feels threatening, dreadful. Our pregnancy seemed interminable, and yet we didn't want it to end. We were alive, but suffering.

We found it helpful to remember that God's people have usually lived here. We are all in a liminal space as we look forward to the new creation. We are saved, but we have not yet gone to be with our Lord. Our suffering will come to an end, but it has not ended yet. Jesus knew that we would be here in this strange space, and he told us how to cope with it: by abiding in his words.

In John 15, as the disciples faced the imminent loss of Jesus himself, Jesus likened them (and us) to branches on a vine. The vine, which represents Jesus, nourishes and gives life to the branches; the branches simply find their life in the vine, and bear the vine's fruit.

I am the vine; you are the branches. Whoever abides in me and I in him, he it is that bears much fruit, for apart from me you can do nothing. (John 15 v 5)

Abiding is not a one-off activity. We don't abide a few times a week, like we might go to the shops or the pool. Abiding is constant; it's like "dwelling". Think of the old-fashioned word "abode", which means "home". Jesus is calling his people to *dwell* in him. Yes, there will be a kind of ebb and flow to how alive and fruitful we feel. But if we are following Jesus, we are invited to listen to him and trust him 24/7.

Day after day you will awake, perhaps terrified of what the next hours may hold. And day after day you can abide in Jesus. You can speak the words of Scripture with God's people down through time: "The steadfast love of the LORD never ceases; his mercies never come to an end; they are new every morning" (Lamentations 3 v 22-23). And you can pray short prayers asking for God's kindness to help you get out of bed and make a coffee—or whatever the very first step of the day might be. You might get out a journal or write on a piece of paper a single Bible verse to keep in your pocket and look at through the day. It doesn't have to be much—just a word, a phrase, something you've found helpful in the past. Perhaps the same few words every day and the same simple prayer. Anything that will help you abide in Jesus.

And on the day goes. Take it minute by minute, hour by hour. In the evening, look back and see how there has indeed been grace carrying you through the day. Here you are, still going by the mercy of God, the one who chose you and will not let you go (John 15 v 16; 10 v 29). Abiding—dwelling—in Jesus, even in this in-between space, by feeding on his words.

LOST FOR WORDS
With all this going on, we also need to navigate relationships with other people whose understanding of what's happening to us or whose experience of life does not match our own.

Awkwardness here is actually not always a bad thing. Sometimes it's the mark of people trying to show love and compassion, but clumsily. This is seen in lots of areas of church life. Someone new walks in and you try to talk to them and welcome them, awkwardly trying to know what to ask and say to put them at ease and find common ground. A non-Christian friend asks you a question about Christianity, and you fumble over the right words to explain clearly why you believe what you believe.

Or you hear that a couple in church are pregnant but that there are major problems with the baby's development. You see they're sitting right next to you. You want them to know how heartbroken you are for them, but aren't sure they'd like you to mention it at all. You ask if they'd like a coffee from the back of church. She's clearly trying to hold back tears and looking down at the floor. He just says, "No thanks, we're ok". Even with the best of intentions, it's awkward.

If you feel awkward around neighbours, friends and church family members who don't understand what you're going through or aren't sure what to say, remember that these difficult interactions are often a sign of care. People are not fluent in this—who possibly could be? Awkwardness is often the zone of truth, and humanness, and self-giving effort.

One of the Bible's most famous passages has this to say about love:

Love is patient and kind ... it is not irritable or resentful ... Love bears all things ... endures all things.
(1 Corinthians 13 v 4-7)

A commitment to love is a commitment to endure awkwardness with patience and kindness—and this applies to us as sufferers as much as it applies to those whose attempts to love us sometimes go awry.

One thing that helped us to act with patience and kindness was having a few very simple conversational "scripts" ready. For instance, when passing strangers congratulated us on Anna's bump, we would smile and accept their congratulations with a "thanks"—seeking to love them and prevent awkwardness on their part. We would not share that it was a twin pregnancy, or the burdensome information about Jed's prognosis. (Our girls, however, had no such compunction: if they were around when a poor, unsuspecting stranger complimented Anna on her bump, the stranger would receive a matter-of-fact, "There are two boys in there but one of them is going to die." This was usually followed by gaping and scrambling for words by the stranger and some serious explaining by Anna or Dan. It shouldn't have been funny but the girls' straightforwardness about the situation sometimes brought a wry smile to our lips.)

To others who clearly wanted to talk more, we'd say: "Thank you. Actually, we're having twin boys. But sadly, one of them has got really major health problems. He's not expected to live, although we're praying that he will." Sometimes we were given opportunities to talk about how our faith in Jesus was transforming our experience of the dark valley.

When people at church asked us how we were doing, but we didn't feel we had the emotional energy to go into lots of detail there and then, we would say: "Thanks. We've been up and down, to be honest, but God's grace has been sufficient every single day. We really appreciate your prayers."

Knowing what we'd say in advance meant we had a short, simple, honest answer to give. It didn't shut the conversation down, but neither did it require people to hold a long conversation that neither they nor us were quite prepared for. We found that people—friends and strangers alike—usually showed touching levels of human compassion for us, for which we were so grateful. We learned that a small step of honesty and vulnerability on our part helped others to relate in a human and vulnerable way in turn.

Usually, but not always. What about the bizarre, trite, or outright offensive comments people sometimes make? At least a couple of people said (almost word for word), "Of course he's going to live—you just need to be positive!" We came to realise that such people were not intending to be profoundly insensitive. They were, nevertheless, blindly selfish. Such a comment is really about not having to engage with the painful and awkward reality you're confronted with. For some people, it is just more comfortable to continue believing that, with enough positivity, all of life can be controlled. The first such comment left us speechless. After that, we were less surprised and were able to end the conversation with a polite "Thank you. We're definitely praying all the time." You never know how people reflect afterwards. One person later came to us and said, "I'm so sorry for how I reacted when you first told me about Jed's problems. I really didn't know what to say and just said the first thing that came into my head."

We were surprised and blessed at how, with a few people, us sharing what was going on with us led them to share their own personal experiences of the loss of a child. For some, this was the loss of their baby many decades prior. Others shared how they had had a sibling who had died in childhood, and what a lasting impact that had had on their whole life into adulthood. Others shared how awful the experience of having a stillborn child had been, such that they would rarely mention it even to close friends. We have been humbled to realise how many people all around us are marked in some way by the tragedy of the loss of a child. We have been blessed with some wonderfully enriched friendships through people's kind willingness to share their own stories with us, after hearing our own little honest summary.

OUR SOLID SAVIOUR

A boy is at death's door with a fever. Realising his son is about to die, the father, a royal official, treks about 18 miles to beg Jesus to come and heal his son. But instead of accompanying the father back to his home, Jesus just says, "Go; your son will live" (John 4 v 46-54). What a staggeringly trite and insensitive thing to say—unless Jesus speaks the truth. Sure enough, the father trails home to find that his son was healed at the very moment that Jesus spoke.

Jesus' response initially seems awkward, jarring: it isn't what the father wanted. But Jesus' words turn out to be solid, true and sure—as they do again and again across the Gospels. Jesus' words are not always what we want to hear, but they are always true. We can abide and live in them.

We began this chapter by recognising that to have a child with severe health problems is to be constantly confronted by your lack of control. The Bible's invitation to us is to leave behind our desperate need to control, and to rest in the love of our Father, who is good. To live in the liminal zone in real time as we keep abiding in the words of Jesus. To love others even when what they say stings.

Part of the ache of suffering is that it can't quite be "weighed" or quantified in any objective way; this is the lament of Job, who suffered terribly (Job 6 v 2-3). There is no clear, consistent, easy way to communicate to others just what a burden we are carrying. It's not like sharing the price of petrol, or the current temperature outside. But although our suffering cannot be adequately articulated, it can be known— and it is known by the Father of our Lord Jesus Christ, the most dependable person in the universe.

The very same voice of Jesus that spoke outrageous hope to the father in John 4 promises to wipe away every tear from his people's eyes. He declares: "Behold, I am making all things new!" (Revelation 21 v 5). We will return to this glorious hope in the final chapter.

3. Walking the Valley

For those reeling from recent loss

We spent six months of pregnancy struggling with the uncertainty of what Jed's life and death would be like. The consultant who had performed our fortnightly pregnancy scans was reasonably confident that Jed's lungs were too small to sustain him, but acknowledged that there was a small chance of hope. We knew that in addition to his small lungs, he would be born with kidney failure, a huge abdomen because of his massive bladder, and deformities of his limbs because of the lack of amniotic fluid surrounding him.

In the end, Jed lived for 24 days, all of them in a neonatal intensive-care incubator. Each day was precious, and each day was difficult. Jed needed to be intubated as soon as he was born and his underdeveloped lungs popped numerous times, requiring painful chest drains. Anna was able to have a treasured cuddle with both boys on their first day but after this, one of our heartaches was that we were unable to hold Jed due to the difficulty of managing his chest drains and breathing tube. Jed underwent two attempts at surgery to overcome the abnormalities in his kidneys and bladder, but his anatomy was so unusual that it wasn't possible.

We are so grateful for the faultless care that Jed received. But three weeks in, it became clear that his body was not able to sustain him. Jed was moved into a side room and kept on a ventilator for the weekend so that we could spend final time with him. He was honoured by visits from wider family, church family and friends. His siblings, Lois, Esther and Ethan, who had been visiting throughout, got to spend longer with him.

The afternoon on which Jed died is truly one of the richest and most precious memories we have. His breathing tube was removed at lunchtime, and for the next four hours we cuddled him in the quietness of our hospital cubicle. He would drift in and out of sleep, repeatedly opening his eyes and gazing at us as we gazed down at him. The actual moment of his death was ever so peaceful.

We cried a lot of tears on that afternoon, but those tears were *mixed*. Tears of terrible grief and loss, mixed with tears of tremendous gratitude, mixed with tears of glorious hope and even tears of joy. The next morning we messaged family and friends, saying, "Jed died looking into our faces, and awoke to Jesus". It was a very sad day for us, but a very glorious one for him.

This chapter is for those in the valley of death. Perhaps a scan has revealed a miscarriage or stillbirth. Perhaps something totally unexpected and utterly dreadful occurred during delivery or shortly after. Perhaps you are reeling from the news of a terrible accident that snatched away your son or daughter. Perhaps the long road of treatment against a cruel disease has ended not in cure, but in death.

Perhaps you are frozen, stunned, numb. Perhaps you are

screaming, or your agitation is beyond expression. Perhaps your body is physically sick in some way as you reel. Perhaps the tears are flowing. In this chapter we would like to invite you, in the midst of your own grief, to weep mixed tears. Beyond the tears of grief, we would like for you to glimpse tears of hope for tomorrow, tears of joy at the age to come, and tears of gratitude. This mixture may well sound impossible even to imagine. But please would you let us explain what we mean—even if that means reading on for just a minute or two at a time?

OUR GUIDE THROUGH THE VALLEY

Psalm 23, probably the most famous psalm in the whole Bible, will be our guide through this chapter. Here's how it begins—speaking of the blessedness of being in a right relationship with God:

> *The LORD is my shepherd; I shall not want.*
> *He makes me lie down in green pastures.*
> *He leads me beside still waters.*
> *He restores my soul.*
> *He leads me in paths of righteousness*
> *for his name's sake. (Psalm 23 v 1-3)*

The next verse is the crucial one for us as we begin to face what has happened. It claims that those who know the Lord as their Shepherd are never alone, not even in death:

> *Even though I walk through the valley*
> *of the shadow of death,*
> *I will fear no evil,*
> *for you are with me;*
> *your rod and your staff,*
> *they comfort me. (v 4)*

This verse begs questions. Why will I not fear the valley of death? How can I know that God is with me? How can I have what Psalm 23 talks about? Jesus is the definitive answer to these questions. Psalm 23 was written about a thousand years before Jesus came, but it is really about him; he had this psalm in mind when he told us that he is "the Good Shepherd" (John 10 v 11). Jesus is the one who protects and comforts us with his rod and staff. How do we know? Because he went there before us.

JESUS IN THE VALLEY

Consider the Bible's accounts of Jesus in the Garden of Gethsemane on the night before his crucifixion. Here is Jesus, the Good Shepherd, going into the valley of death. The burden of awful emotional stress was real, and he experienced that strain fully. We are told that his sweat was "like great drops of blood falling down to the ground" (Luke 22 v 44). Jesus was experiencing something later described by medics as *haematohidrosis*: a rare symptom reported during situations of extreme emotional distress (such as warfare), in which the small blood vessels within sweat glands burst, mixing blood into sweat. Jesus truly *felt* the awful weight of his experience.

The Good Shepherd went into the valley of death—and died. That might be surprising if we're expecting a shepherd who conducts us safely through the valley of death. What good does it do us?

All the good in the world. Jesus suffered and died *for us*. When Jesus was condemned, a guilty rebel and murderer named Barabbas was freed. It's a small picture of what actually happened on Jesus' cross: he *swapped* with us. The Good Shepherd went into the valley of death and died for us, his sheep. He took our place and brought us acceptance, pardon, and the knowledge of God's love.

But this is not all. After Jesus died, he rose. And he ascended to heaven and sat down on God's throne to rule over all things. Enthroned in heaven, he poured out the promised Holy Spirit, who is God's personal empowering presence. All those who trust in Jesus receive the Holy Spirit, who works particularly to comfort God's people and to empower us to endure hard things patiently—and even joyfully—as we trust in God the Father. Jesus died to bring us life, and to give us the Holy Spirit.

With this in mind, we can see that Jesus has put flesh on Psalm 23:

- "The LORD is my shepherd". A shepherd faces danger on behalf of his sheep. Jesus suffered and died *for* us: he is the Shepherd who leads and cares for us at the utmost cost to himself.
- "Even though I walk through the valley of the shadow of death, I will fear no evil". Jesus was raised to life: he has defeated death and lives for ever and ever (Revelation 1 v 18). So he rules over the valley of death.
- "For you are with me". Jesus poured out the promised Holy Spirit: God himself dwells within us by his Spirit to comfort us in the darkest valleys of our experience. Jesus' people are *never alone*.

And so Psalm 23 becomes true of us. We can say that we need not fear evil, because Jesus has *conquered* and rules over it. And we can say that he is always with us, because we have his Spirit.

This changes the fear with which we face the death of a child. If we know Jesus, we no longer need desperately to try to control or even understand a situation far beyond our grasp. Instead, we can pour out our hearts to King Jesus in the midst of the pain, knowing three things:

1. *That he sympathises—literally, he "suffers with" us. He knows pain, loss and suffering to the greatest extent. Our King has wounds. He fully inhabits the experience of the broken-hearted and crushed in spirit.*
2. *That he rules over death itself. This doesn't answer all our questions, but knowing his heart and his power does mean we can trust him in the valley.*
3. *That he is personally present by his Spirit with us right now, to comfort us.*

When we "live inside" Psalm 23, through Jesus, we can weep mixed tears—tears of grief along with tears of hope, gratitude and even joy. As we're about to see.

TEARS OF GRIEF

For us, on the afternoon when Jed died, we were able to be fully present to the situation, crying tears of grief towards our Lord Jesus. If we didn't know Jesus was *in control*, we would have been distracted, restlessly trying to do more to fix, solve, control and understand. And if we didn't know that Jesus himself has *wounds*, we wouldn't have cried openly to him. King Jesus enables us to grieve truly as human beings in the valley of death.

TEARS OF HOPE FOR TOMORROW

Psalm 23 concludes like this:

You prepare a table before me
in the presence of my enemies;

> *you anoint my head with oil;*
> *my cup overflows.*
> *Surely goodness and mercy shall follow me*
> *all the days of my life,*
> *and I shall dwell in the house of the LORD*
> *for ever. (v 5-6)*

The image we're given is itself mixed. On the one hand, it's an abundant banquet where your cup "overflows". But at the same time, it's a context of threat, trouble, darkness and grief: the banquet happens "in the presence of my enemies". In other words, the experience of Jesus' people is one of being comforted and cared for by him in the broken here and now, whilst also savouring the glorious hope of what is finally to come.

The word for "mercy" here can be translated with a wide array of English phrases—loving-kindness, steadfast love and unfailing love. It's God's promise-keeping love. It's his "I've said it so I'll definitely do it" love; his unbreakably loyal love. We don't have a good English word for it. The point is that Jesus' people rest secure in God's love for them, not because they are lovable, not even because God feels sorry for them, but because God has promised to love his people for ever— and he always keeps his promises. And he has proven this in Jesus becoming a man and going to the cross to die. Every time we look to Jesus' cross, the unbreakably loyal love of God is shown to us.

This is not a love which, strictly speaking, "follows" us. It does not lag distantly behind, keeping lazy track of us. Biblical Hebrew has an "intensive" form of verbs—used here in Psalm 23 v 6 to denote that God's goodness and mercy don't so much *follow* us as *pursue* us. King Jesus, the King with wounds, won for his people the eternal security of knowing the love of God. It's why the Bible can say that *nothing* can separate us from the love of God which is in Christ Jesus (Romans 8 v 38-39).

Here is what we are trying to say: even in the darkest valleys and seasons, those who trust in Jesus can know that his love will pursue us, even when (especially when) we cannot see any way ahead. Those who trust in Jesus will find that each new day will have new mercy. We cannot store up and stockpile the mercies of God; rather, we can trust that tomorrow's woes will have tomorrow's grace. How can we be sure of this? Behold your King! Jesus is the ever-flowing fountain of the life and love of the Father. His self-giving love shown at the cross assures us. The New Testament is emphatic that Jesus is alive and reigning over all things *for his church* (e.g. Ephesians 1 v 19-23). So our tears can be mixed with both grief for today and hope for tomorrow.

TEARS OF JOY IN THE COMING AGE

There's still more. We can cry tears of joy as we see the resurrection. Jesus' death is not only the way in which the love of the Father is revealed, and it is not only the way that all our sins are forgiven. Jesus' death marks the putting to death of the whole broken order of things. In Jesus' death, *death itself* was put to death. Jesus' resurrection has guaranteed a final end to death, and the certainty of unbroken life dwelling in a whole new creation. This is what Psalm 23 is rejoicing in when it ends, "I shall dwell in the house of the Lord for ever".

The Bible gives a picture of God storing up our tears, in our nights of sorrow, in a bottle (Psalm 56 v 8). Revelation 21 v 4 says that one day Jesus will wipe every tear from our eyes. We might think of him taking our bottled tears off the shelf and leaving us speechless with joy at how they are wiped away, how they are erased.

With some griefs, we can vaguely imagine how God might comfort us. But many leave us dumbfounded as to why God allowed such loss. You may be sceptical that God ever could wipe such tears away, that he could ever remove the pain. But the cross of Jesus—which, remember, is the display of the Father's love—invites us to trust that God has ways that are simply outside of our predicting; unexpected and painful, yet better than we could ever imagine. Those who wait on the Lord will not be disappointed.

For now, we weep in the valley of death—but as we look to the future there is another kind of tear mixed into our weeping. It is truly the teardrop of unspeakable joy.

TEARS OF GRATITUDE

With all the above in mind, we were able to cry tears of *gratitude*. Throughout our pregnancy, then Jed's life and the grieving afterwards, we have tried to make a habit of tracing out the contours of the Lord's grace to us in the midst of the bitterness of the season. Whenever one of us is tempted to dwell on what fun Jed would be having with his twin brother, Ethan, we remind one another, "There is no joy to be found there", and we turn to gratitude instead. It's not always easy; we have got better with practice.

Can you see ways in which Jesus has revealed himself to you as a tender Shepherd? Anna often shares that, although she had trusted in Jesus for many years, she frankly struggled to *feel affection* for him. Tasting the Lord's kindness in this season really warmed her heart to her Saviour, and for that she is truly thankful. This might not be your experience—

sometimes in our grief Jesus feels very far away. But perhaps there is one Bible verse that has comforted you, or one prayer that has spoken to you? Or perhaps there is some way in which you can reach out to Jesus, far away though he seems, and ask for his help to love him more. Write down your prayer and watch for the answer—then give thanks for it.

Can you be thankful for the love of others who have walked alongside you? Are there any relationships that have deepened? Have you had conversations in which you have been able to speak honestly about your faith and your hope for the future?

What can you give thanks for in the life of the child you lost—however short it was? We were so grateful that Jed lived long enough for us to meet him face to face. You may be grateful for experiences you had while pregnant, or for memories you made with your child.

You might like to try making a list of things that you are thankful for, to which you can return in the darkest moments. Deliberately remembering these things directs our attention towards gratitude.

The journey through death is awful and tear-filled. But Jesus enables us to cry mixed tears: tears of bitter loss, tears of hope and confidence in his care to carry us tomorrow and the next day, tears of longing joy, and tears of gratitude. Why not take a few minutes now to read through Psalm 23 again? If the tears come, don't stop them. Ask God to help you cry mixed tears as you remember Jesus, the Good Shepherd.

PRACTICAL POSTSCRIPT:
ADVICE FOR THE EARLY DAYS OF GRIEF

Express your grief:

- You might consider writing in some way. This might be a personal journal. You could literally scribble a single word each day, finding that on occasion this gives rise to a flow of expression of grief.
- You might consider reading through the Psalms, perhaps with a Scripture journal version, and pausing every time you reach a verse which expresses some of the grief and longing you are feeling. Underline those and spend as much time as you need with them.
- If you have other children, cry with them and share honestly with them. They can handle it. The ones who can't handle it are us parents; we can't handle the loss of control. We can't handle being seen as weak in our children's eyes. Let us model not strength but weakness. You can show little ones how you lean on Jesus while you cry.
- Doing what you can to involve others in the wider family will prove to be a great help to you all down the line. Your own parents, wider family and friends will be grieving the loss in their own ways, whilst not wanting to burden you.

Remember:

- Take as many photos and videos as you feel able to. We treasure every photo of Jed. If there are young children involved, such as siblings or cousins of the child who died, photos will be ever so important to them. Similarly, if you have a child later on, he or she will in time dearly want to learn about the brother or sister who died before their birth.

- Encourage grieving children to draw, record videos or photos, and generally make any memories they can. Losing a sibling will be a deeply precious and indelible part of their identity. Do all you can to involve them and provide them with space and memories.

Simplify communication:

- The sheer volume of messaging is something which needs recognising and navigating. It can exhaust you. You may find it helpful to create an email list or WhatsApp broadcast in order to send updates to all your family and friends. If there is someone who can do this on your behalf, even better.
- You might consider coming off social media altogether. The detrimental effects of social media on mental health are doubly devastating in a season of grief. The last thing you want when you have lost a child is for your phone to notify you about your acquaintances' flippant or thoughtless posts, or to show you streams of pictures of healthy babies and happy families.
- Walk closely with a few in church. This is likely to be a time when your relational capacity is vastly reduced. But if you have one or two people who will listen, who will be there, who are committed to walking with you, then you are blessed.

Get space:

- Clear as much as you can from your head and your schedule. Grief requires space. As far as possible, ask others to take things off your plate. This is not being lazy. This is the humility to recognise that there are times in life where we just need to be able to breathe and let the dust settle. Accept that you are wounded. If there are kind people offering to help us, say yes.

- Through the generosity of family and friends, we were able (along with three-week-old Ethan) to spend two nights away together in a lovely coastal hotel a few days after Jed's death. After the rollercoaster of Jed's hospital stay and the emotion of his death, it was a truly welcome change of space and pace. If it is at all possible for you, please consider this.

Accept help:

- Supporting services around child loss are worth connecting with. Through the neonatal unit in which Jed was cared for, we were put in touch with social workers, psychologists, and more. If nothing else, knowing the support is there is a great help. For some of us, the thought that we might ever need a social worker or psychologist threatens our pride. A major grief shows you how vulnerable you are to having your whole life fall apart. Attentive listening is not always easy to come by, so if you have the chance to speak with a therapist or psychologist after losing a child you are unlikely to regret it. Similarly, you may be surprised about how helpful a social worker's recommendations and suggestions prove to be. A one percent easing can make all the difference.

4. After the Storm

For those continuing to grieve

Do you know what it's like to hang by a thread? To feel like even the slightest extra strain will break you entirely?

Dan remembers one Saturday morning taking our girls for a walk to the supermarket to buy a treat for breakfast, and to give Anna and newborn Ethan (Jed's twin brother) a slightly quieter morning. It was a few weeks after Jed had died. They had to walk there because our car had developed a fault and needed repairs. They chose some pastries and went to pay for them. Dan's bank card was declined. He tried another card, which was declined too. In the end they put some food back, and bought just what the single pound coin in Dan's wallet could buy. That Saturday morning was spent on the phone to our card companies trying to discover what the problem was. It turned out that, since we had bought a new pushchair the night before from an online seller we hadn't previously used, our card had been frozen as an anti-fraud measure. The other card was declined simply because we hadn't used it in so long. By the end of the morning Dan could barely speak with frustration and sheer exhaustion. Jed had died, the car was broken, and now our bank cards were being declined.

This might sound simply like an unfortunate Saturday morning; people suffer far worse. But we can tell you that we were at breaking point; emotionally gasping for air. Anything further was going to suck us into a black hole.

This chapter is for people who live in the awful silence after a terrible loss; sufferers who peer into the future and find it now to be blank, bleak, a frozen and numbing wasteland. "Life after the storm" is maybe the wrong metaphor. The storm doesn't suddenly end with a quick return to warm, sunny days—the rainy, grey conditions can linger, fluctuating in intensity. Maybe the loss happened two weeks ago. Maybe two years ago. We will never move on from this. But we will move on *with* this.

This chapter is mostly a practical look at moving on with grief. To begin, let's ponder these precious words:

As a father shows compassion to his children,
*   so the L*ORD* shows compassion to those who fear him.*
For he knows our frame;
*   he remembers that we are dust. (Psalm 103 v 13-14)*

This passage is one of many which speak of God's tenderness, and so when we are hanging by a thread it's right that we come here. Here we are assured that he has fatherly compassion towards us; and that he knows our frailty.

All these things are not abstract ideas about what God *might* be like; they are unmistakably shown in Jesus. In his life and death, Jesus shows us the compassion of God. Again and again, Jesus is tender towards human frailty. In fact, Jesus himself knows the full extent of human weakness. You may know the account of Jesus asleep in a boat, even though a furious storm has broken out (Matthew 8 v 24): he knows exhaustion. You may know of Jesus hanging on the cross, bleeding and thirsty, and calling out, "My God, my God, why have you forsaken me?" (Matthew 27 v 46). Jesus has fully inhabited the life of sufferers. And so when we suffer we have fellowship with Jesus. He knows that "we are dust".

EMBRACING DUSTINESS

When the Bible says that humans were created "from the dust of the ground" (Genesis 2 v 7 NIV), the point is that we are *physically made*. Modern science is saying something completely consistent with the Bible when it discovers and describes the cells, molecules, hormones, clotting cascades, neurotransmitters and more which comprise our bodies: we are *essentially physical*.

On the other hand, modern science fundamentally disagrees with the Bible if it claims that these things are in themselves what make you alive. The very same verse says that God himself breathed (or spirited) into us the "breath (or spirit) of life", and at that point we became living beings. We are dust, but we are dust which has been *made to live*.

Think of a musical instrument. On the one hand, a violin is an undeniably physical item, made of wood and other materials. On the other hand, it plays music. The music is sounded by physical molecules, yet it isn't defined by them. Music depends on the physicality of the instrument, whilst music itself isn't limited to those molecules—you could play the same music on a different instrument, or through an mp3 file or an old vinyl. Musical instruments and music are related but distinct. And here's the key part of the metaphor: the better the instrument is cared for, the better the manifestation of the music.

In the same way, our bodies are physical, "the dust of the ground". And our experience flows *through* our molecules and neurotransmitters, including our spiritual journey of faith and joy in Jesus Christ. It's not that physical stuff is an illusion. Nor is it that physical is bad, primitive, something to be escaped from. Our spiritual existence flows inseparably through our physical "dust", like music flows through the physicality of an instrument. The better we care for the physical reality of our bodies, the better the quality of human experience.

This always matters, but it matters more than ever for those who grieve. The stress and exhaustion of grief has profound physical consequences for our bodies and brains, and thus for our emotions. As we will reflect below, this can show itself in a host of ways. Anger, relational disconnectedness and workaholism can be just as much a symptom as tears and sadness.

We ignore our "dustiness" to our peril. To summarise:

1. *If you have experienced a massive loss such as the death of your child, this will have unavoidable effects on your brain and body, and thus your emotions.*
2. *God compassionately knows that we are dust.*
3. *Therefore, the way ahead involves **accepting** our "dustiness" and leaning into the fact that the Father of our Lord Jesus knows and cares for us as we are.*

PARTICULAR SHAPES OF GRIEF

Everyone's journey in grief is unique. Yet there are common shapes and contours to our "dustiness" which many of us will experience. Don't be surprised if you meet these:

Mothers:

The dear mother of the child who has died lives at the very epicentre of this profound loss. Life may now overflow with tears, numbness, and a resigned inability to invest in anything that requires emotion. On top of this, persistent dark thoughts of self-blame may hound you. *Is God punishing me because I sinned? If only I hadn't XYZ, then this would never have happened.* It can feel impossible to put certain questions to bed. Some of us will virtually stop eating. Others will binge. You might feel tired all the time—either sleeping 14 hours a day or lying awake, exhausted, vigilant, through the hours of the night. If you have other children, you may become obsessively anxious for their safety; you just cannot bear the thought of losing them too. This is indeed a dark valley. *But our Father looks on us with never-ending compassion.*

Fathers:

A common challenge for dear fathers stumbling through grief is to try to become functional too fast. We want to be back at work; we want to be the one who can fix things for our wife and children. We carry shame from feeling we are not enough as husbands and fathers, since we carry a lurking pressure upon ourselves to be heroes. For many men, being depressed shows itself not so much in tears but in disconnectedness, and in addictive behaviours which put a brief covering over our inner shame. These can include workaholism, gambling, pornography, alcohol, eating, exercise (a positive thing, as we'll see below, but nevertheless something we can use as an addictive covering for our grief), and more. Why does shame feature so highly in the journey on with grief? Because we constantly feel confronted with our powerlessness; we are unavoidably out of our depth; we are unable to be what we think our wives and children need. You may lack the energy and drive you once had at work, or find yourself dropping the ball. You may become irritable and angry—and then deeply disappointed in yourself. *But our Father knows we are dust, and so we are loved as we flounder. Our Lord Jesus is the hero, not us.*

Marriage:

Losing a child can place enormous stress on a marriage. One of the wisest things we can do is acknowledge this fully. For a start, even the healthiest and happiest marriages experience strain at times, even when there's no grief anywhere. What makes a marriage healthy is not the absence of strain or conflict, but the capacity for repeated healthy resolution. Yet when we carry grief, our capacity is drastically *decreased.* This includes our emotional and relational capacity. What this can mean is that healthy communication feels exhaustingly difficult. We might stop having conversations with our spouse; or conversations now involve one person barely participating. On top of this, when we carry grief, our emotional needs are drastically *increased,* and are far more complex and tender. Grief decreases our capacity and increases our need. In short, when a married couple grieve together it can become enormously hard for them to listen, love and comfort one another in the very season when listening, loving, and comforting is what they desperately need. *But as we both lean on Jesus, we will find his compassion is always enough to bear us up and enable us to love one another.*

On top of all of this, losing a child is an unavoidable, indelible grief etched into your marriage. It is an unalterable part of the fabric and shared story that binds you and your spouse. Whatever used to be our common history, and our shared outlook to the future, losing our child is now among the biggest factors. For this reason, sharing a major grief will alter a marriage in one way or the other. Please be aware of the tragic route this can take: your spouse can become an unavoidable reminder of grief, and thus someone you eventually feel you need distance from. But it doesn't have to be that way. Through the hard and sad work of metabolising this shared grief together, the gospel can knit us closer at a more vulnerable and truly human level than ever before. *We can keep going to Jesus together.*

Siblings and parenting:

For brothers and sisters who have lost their sibling, grief may be experienced, stored and expressed in cryptic ways, especially if they are young. Little ones are vividly sensitive, yet with far fewer means of expressing what they feel. Thus, the two-year-old may have inexplicable tantrums or need constant consoling. Older children may attempt to internalise their grief, intuitively trying not to add to their parents' worries, only for this to manifest itself in some surprise way down the line. As with marriage, you may find that your parental headspace is so drastically diminished that you struggle as parents in ways you never used to. You may find yourself feeling ashamed as you struggle to understand or accept how hard you are finding basic daily life. *But our God is the true, unfailing Father of pure, unfailing compassion and we rest in him. We can be "great parents" only when we depend greatly on God our Father.*

Grandparents:

Our co-author Chris, who writes in chapter 6 about the death of his son, has also known the pain of the tragic death of two of his grandchildren. He wrote to us, "When my children are undergoing trauma, my first impulse is to wish it was happening to me instead. As parents, we often hurt more when our kids are in pain than if we were experiencing the pain ourselves. Consequently, when our 3-year-old grandson died unexpectedly, not only did I have my own grief to process stemming from my own relationship with him, I had the added and more intense distress of processing my daughter's grief." *But God knows our frailties and the complexities of our distress. Once again, we can be "great parents" to our adult children only when we depend greatly on God our Father.*

Church:
Without anyone intending it, going to church can be daunting. The thought of countless people asking how you are can be exhausting. On the other hand, if you go to church and people *don't* ask you how you're doing (perhaps out of awkwardness), you might feel devastated at the "fakeness" of Christians who believe in a compassionate and relational God yet can't or won't engage with those who grieve. If you're relatively new at your church, now probably feels like a difficult time to get started with telling people your story. For all of us there is this paradox with church: we fear facing lots of people when we are hurting most. Yet when we are hurting is when we most need people. *Church is primarily about God, not about other people. When churches open up their Bibles week after week, the God of grace is proclaimed—near to the broken-hearted, strengthener of the weary. We need constant sight of God the hope-giver.*

Finally, would you let us share one warning? The darkest side of grief is not its impact on your mood, sleep, energy or relationships. The darkest and most subtle side is an enslaving lie that can creep in and be believed. And that lie is: "This terrible suffering now defines who I am. I am a victim, and nothing will change that."

It is at root a lie because the Bible doesn't give us an entitlement to children. If we believe we are entitled to children, then if we cannot have them, or lose them to death, we feel robbed. It is tempting to wrap that belief around us as a kind of cocoon. But ultimately what it becomes is a tragic kind of self-righteousness that keeps you from true connection with others, from connection with yourself, and most of all from experiencing the grace of God in Jesus. The way through this consists not in nurturing resentment and blame, but in *actively choosing* to keep looking to God in the pain.

Grief is a miserable journey. Perhaps you are experiencing all of the above and much more besides. But as we have seen, there are wonderful truths about God to sustain us as we hang by a thread. At the end of the chapter you will find some practical suggestions for moving on with grief in everyday life. But first let us return to Jesus.

A STRANGE BLESSING

To live after the storm of major loss is to tread the long route of mourning. We've seen that God knows and has compassion on our "dustiness". In the New Testament Jesus puts it far more strongly:

Blessed are those who mourn. (Matthew 5 v 4)

We gratefully receive God's compassion as we mourn. But how can Jesus call us *blessed*?

Because those who mourn see things as they are; the true

frailty, fragility, and finitude of human existence. Human pride is instantly melted by grief.

Because those who mourn are thus better prepared to see and enjoy God.

Because those who come to know God as he truly is will find themselves comforted beyond their dreams.

> *Blessed are those who mourn,* **for they shall be comforted**. *(Matthew 5 v 4)*

Jesus elsewhere says something very similar: "Blessed are you who weep now, for you shall laugh" (Luke 6 v 21). The overall idea in these passages is that everyone who thought they were at the very bottom of the hill will find they're really at the very top, in the great reversal of things that comes through Jesus' death and resurrection. Our English word "blessed" doesn't quite map the concept. It's the sense of happy, fortunate, the good life. Jesus is saying that those who mourn in him actually have the good life. To see why, let's spend a bit of time unpacking the three "because" statements above.

Those who mourn actually have the opportunity of a clearer and purer line of sight at the glory of Jesus, since the distracting cobwebs of daily life have been painfully pulled away. Grief makes us forget our grand plans, our restless activity, our petty squabbles. Now all we have is the glory of the love of God. And, difficult though it may be to believe this right now, the more you gaze at God's glory, the more you will find that it is all you need. It becomes all you want.

What do we really mean by this? "Glory" can seem a vague and foggy word. What it means is the greatness of someone or something. It's what you admire. We admire giraffes for their long necks; blue whales for their size; an Olympic athlete for their speed or strength. And God? All his works show his glory. We admire him for his beauty and wisdom in creation; in sunsets and freshly fallen snow. But his most distinctive, personal glory is shown in his self-giving love. This is most clearly shown in Jesus' giving himself to death on his cross. It's why Jesus speaks, especially in John's Gospel, of being "glorified" as the cross comes into view (e.g., John 12 v 23-33). Jesus' death for us on the cross is our greatest glimpse of God's glory.

God, who is love, loved a people from eternity past and saved them completely through the blood of his Son and the outpouring of his Spirit. All this is "to the praise of his glory" (Ephesians 1 v 12, 14). In other words, *we admire and adore him for it.*

Can we invite you to pause and think about this? You may feel you are hanging by a thread; you are deeply aware of your "dustiness". But God sees you and has compassion on you. He has intervened in history for you. He has sent his Son to die for you and his Spirit to live inside you. His love for you is the clearest demonstration of his nature. This is your God! And there is nothing that can stop this being true—nothing that can separate you from this love.

This then is how we are comforted. Those who are devastated and powerless with grief can do nothing but gaze at the glory of God. In our past lives we might have spoken about "glorifying God" by our own actions—but now, grounded by grief and deeply aware of our own weaknesses, we realise that we glorify God not by doing great things for him but by knowing and trusting him *as he really is*. We glorify a chef not by trying to cook a meal for her, but by enjoying the feast she has prepared for us. We glorify God by feeding on his self-giving love, utterly entrusting ourselves to his care in our darkest seasons. We glorify him—and we find that we are comforted.

KEEP GOING TO JESUS

In heaven, all of Jesus' followers will be full of joy and delight. But the fact that Jesus will "wipe away every tear" from our eyes (Revelation 21 v 4) means that some will be *more comforted* than others, since some have *more tears* to wipe away. Imagine three children who walk home in the pouring rain, arriving freezing cold and miserable. One of them, on the way, falls and cuts themselves painfully. All three children will be comforted by their parent. But the one with the wounds will be more comforted—and know more of their parent's tenderness.

The greater the loss and the mourning, the greater will be the comfort. In the greater pain, we are brought to a greater intimacy with Jesus, since we have a clearer line of sight to his heart. So let this be our resolute, remorseless, returning point in our journey with loss: that if we mourn, we are blessed.

You may not *feel* this right now. Perhaps you are full of questions, fears, anger. Perhaps Jesus feels far away and your love for him is faint. *Where is the comfort, Lord?* you may be asking. But the good news is that hope flows not from you, but from the Father who knows—and cares—that you are dust. You can pray to him even in the darkest moments, even when you are barely clinging to faith or sanity.

The greatest advice we can offer is this: *keep going to Jesus.* He knows how to sustain his weary ones. He knows grief. He knows that we are dust. He walks with us. He will comfort us. And one day, we will roar with laughter, the laughter of a joy unimaginable to us now. Because in Jesus, the path of tears leads unstoppably to the coming age of rejoicing.

PRACTICAL POSTSCRIPT:
ADVICE FOR THE AFTERMATH

Lament:

The Bible's laments prove to be both a comfort and a help. A comfort, because we read and know that we are not alone in our pain. We belong to a God who sees, hears, and knows; and we are surrounded by fellow-sufferers who have walked and wept similar paths before us. And laments are a help since they provide us with words to trace out and make our own, when we are in a place so shattered that the very effort of articulating all that we feel is overwhelming. You'll find a list of laments in Appendix I. Start with Psalm 13. Perhaps copy out a few verses, or the whole thing, by hand. You may find you're able to start writing your own short prayers after a chunk of verses. Keep going. A verse or two a day might seem like nothing, but through the hard and slow months they will compound into shaping the way you think and feel towards God.

Care for your "dust":

Sleep is always important, but now more than ever. If you can, stop setting a morning alarm. But set a "go to bed" alarm, which will help you to get to bed early.

There's a strong argument for cutting out alcohol altogether when you are grieving. Its addictive powers are strong, especially to mourners. And it vastly worsens sleep quality. Similarly, keep caffeine in check. Endless cups of tea or coffee are comforting. But they can disrupt good sleep. Our goal now is not productivity, but recovery: we are dust.

It's so obvious and yet sometimes so difficult to prioritise—nutritious food and regular exercise energise our physical bodies and thus the experience of our embodied souls. Is there a book of easy, healthy recipes you could work through? Could you walk outdoors for half an hour each day (maybe with a friend)?

Allow yourself margin:
As we care for our "dustiness" in the aftermath of grief, let the guiding principle be *margin*: more sleep, more rest, more time, less pressure, fewer decisions. Wherever you can make changes in life, opt for more margin. If you feel uncomfortable with this—you want to be back at full capacity as quickly as you can—then set yourself a reminder 6 months from now (or even better, 12 months). Make a promise with yourself that you're going to focus on margin for the next 6 months, and re-evaluate after that.

If you are in paid employment, take whatever steps are in your power to ease the strain at your place of work. This is a major area of life where the desire to be at full capacity too soon can push you into a place of horrible exhaustion. Is it possible with your employer, and with your own budget, to work a day fewer a week, or have an extra half-day off? Could you take a week of unpaid leave every other month? Would starting late on a couple of mornings a week be possible?

Give extra space for anniversaries. Above all, the anniversary of your child's death, but also their due date or birthday. There will be other significant dates for you no doubt; perhaps the day you learned you were pregnant, or the day of their funeral. As far as possible, plan yourself an easy day. You have nothing to lose if, when it comes, you feel basically fine. You have everything to gain if it proves to be a real low.

For further practical reflections, please see Appendix I.

5. A Short and Precious Life

For those facing the loss of an infant

or unborn baby

Y ou may be reading this because you are pregnant with a child who is not expected to live for long. Or, perhaps you have lost a child, and their life was tragically short. A short life raises painful questions: how can this be anything but a wasteful tragedy? What was the meaning of such a small and short life? We are confronted with the need to make sense of the meaning of life.

We spent much of our pregnancy struggling with tension caused by the uncertainty of what would happen at the end of it. In the end, our Jed lived for just over three weeks, and they were among the most precious weeks of our lives. And in the years since his death, our lives and the lives of those around us have been enriched. Whilst we would long to still have him with us, we are able to *delight* daily in the memory of Jed's life. His life was not a waste. How is this?

In this chapter, we reflect on how it can be possible to delight in a life which was far too short.

INTIMATELY KNOWN

Question: Is a life less *valuable* if it lasts three hours, compared to one which lasts 90 years? Answer: No. (For more on this question about the intrinsic value of life, see chapter 7.)

But what about this question: Is a life less *meaningful* if it lasts three hours rather than 90 years? We pause and ponder this. Those of us who have lost little ones are forced to ponder questions that might never have crossed our minds before.

What is meaning? It's the sum of the connections. A wedding ring on display in a shop might not *mean* much, in that it's a small object, relatively easy to manufacture. But after it is bought and given in marriage, the ring's meaning lies in all that is bound up with it: our wedding rings *mean a lot* to us. In the same way, the meaning of life doesn't lie in its length or function. It lies in the sum of its connections, in the sum of personal, relational knowledge. This is the case even if a person appears not to be aware of it. For instance, an elderly relative may suffer advanced dementia, or be in a coma, and seem unaware of your presence next to them. But they still *mean a great deal* to you. Meaning is not about length of life, but about *being known*.

There are different kinds of knowledge:

- "know-what"—knowing information. For example, facts learned from a history book.
- "know-how'"—learning skills. For example, how to drive a car.
- "know-who"—knowing other people and being known as a person.

"Know-who" is ultimately what gives life meaning. Why do we say this? Because the Bible sets great store on knowing and being known by God the Father. That is the personal knowledge which gives endless richness and meaning to our existence.

The wonder of being *known personally by a personal God* is a big part of the majesty in Psalm 139:

> *O LORD, you have searched me and known me! You know when I sit down and when I rise up; you discern my thoughts from afar. (v 1-2)*

> *Even before a word is on my tongue, behold, O LORD, you know it altogether ... Such knowledge is too wonderful for me. (v 4, 6)*

> *Your eyes saw my unformed substance; in your book were written, every one of them, the days that were formed for me, when as yet there was none of them. How precious to me are your thoughts, O God! How vast is the sum of them! If I would count them, they are more than the sand.*
> *(v 16-18)*

Do you see how, in this psalm, the author (King David) is frankly overwhelmed at the richness of the meaning of his life, existing within the boundless knowledge of God? Meaning is the sum of the connections; and if a human is known by an infinite God, then that connection is immeasurable in meaning. A human life has immeasurable meaning.

This means that a short life has as much meaning as a long life—since the meaning comes from God in relation to the person, not the person in relation to themselves. From the eternal perspective of an infinitely great God, a short and a long life look the same. Their meaning is bound up with being known by him, not in their length of days.

This is an enormous comfort for us who grieve infant loss. In fact, we intuitively grasp this. Since Jed and Ethan were identical twins, and Jed died but Ethan lived, people would try to comfort us, with words like "Well, at least you have one baby." In one sense, of course, this is true. We are unspeakably grateful that we didn't lose both boys. But at the same time, those words feel incredibly callous. Why? Because the meaning of a human life is such that you can't use arithmetic reasoning. A mother who had four children and loses one does not simply then feel like a mother with three children.

Perhaps, as you grieve, you are lamenting the loss of your opportunity to get to know your child, to watch their unique character unfurl. It is a balm for us to know that whilst we lost that opportunity in this life, the personal God of the universe knows them intimately. They are moulded and appreciated by him. Though their time with us in this present age was painfully short, their life was definitely not a waste.

A SHORT LIFE IS *BETTER*

On top of this, the Bible has some quietly spoken surprises for us. There is a very real sense in which a very short life is actually *better* than a long one. A sense in which a baby who dies has a life to envy. Why is that? This can only make sense because of two things:

1. *This age is full of evil.*
2. *There is a life to come.*

And therefore:

3. *To pass quickly through this life into the next, without seeing and suffering evil, is good.*

These ideas are picked up in parts of books of the Bible like Job and Ecclesiastes. These are books which are concerned with *wisdom*; with how we make our way through life with faith in God in the midst of the mess of life *as it really is*. Over the millennia, these are books which have been loved for their capacity to articulate honestly the baffling, ambiguous, grievous, perplexing and mysterious parts of human existence with reference to God. Here is what Job says in the midst of the physical and emotional agony he is suffering:

> *Why did I not die at birth,*
> *   come out from the womb and expire?*
> *Why did the knees receive me?*
> *   Or why the breasts, that I should nurse?*
> *For then I would have lain down and been quiet;*
> *   I would have slept; then I would have been at rest,*
> *with kings and counsellors of the earth*
> *   who rebuilt ruins for themselves,*
> *or with princes who had gold,*
> *   who filled their houses with silver.*
> ***Or why was I not as a hidden stillborn child,***
> ***   as infants who never see the light?***
> *There the wicked cease from troubling,*
> *   and there the weary are at rest. (Job 3 v 11-17)*

He says a similar thing later when he cries out to God:

> *Why did you bring me out from the womb?*
> ***   Would that I had died before any eye had seen me***
> *and were as though I had not been,*
> *   carried from the womb to the grave. (10 v 18-19)*

Job wishes he had died as an infant: that way, he would not have had to experience such evil. And in the Bible, and Christian tradition, Job is not regarded as a man who spoke hastily from a place of pain, but as a *wise man*.

Then there's Ecclesiastes. The author of the book may well have been King Solomon, famed for his great wisdom and insight. In any case, the book is again a tutor in *wisdom*.

> *And I thought the dead who are already dead more fortunate than the living who are still alive. But better than both is he who has not yet been and has not seen the evil deeds that are done under the sun.*
>
> *(Ecclesiastes 4 v 2-3)*

In fact, the original Hebrew is more emphatic than we might realise. The sense is not just that he "thought [the dead] more fortunate"—it's that he praises, he applauds, he massively congratulates those who have already died. Again, the reason is that they either haven't seen, or no longer see, the evil things done under the sun. Ecclesiastes comes back to this theme a little later on:

> *If a man fathers a hundred children and lives many years, so that the days of his years are many, but his soul is not satisfied with life's good things, and he also has no burial, I say that a **stillborn child is better off than he**. For it comes in vanity and goes in darkness, and in darkness its name is covered. Moreover, it has not seen the sun or known anything, yet it finds rest rather than he.*
>
> *(Ecclesiastes 6 v 3-5)*

We may well struggle greatly with this, and that is ok. The point of these books of wisdom is to help us wrestle with big questions, not to give fully rounded and categorical answers. Of course we do not wish a short life on our children; of course there are many good things in life as well as bad ones. Nevertheless, this perspective is helpful in the wake of loss. There *is* a sense in which short lives are more privileged than longer ones, since they haven't seen and suffered the evil of this world.

Recall what we considered first in this chapter, that a short life has just as much meaning as a long one, and you may find that you are in a surprising place. A place where, even in the midst of grief, you are beginning to glimpse how you might delight in, celebrate, and even *be happy* for the one whom you have lost.

For us, this has been a long and repeated journey of turning our routine and received ways of thinking and grieving into a shape which is more biblical:

- We miss Jed each and every day.
- We know that his life, although terribly short—and far too short for us—is just as meaningful as if he had lived for 100 years, since God knows him.
- He's the most blessed member of the family, since he passed very swiftly through this world of war, tears, injustice and abuse. Jed will never have to grieve the loss of a child.

THE GLORY TO BE REVEALED

Despite this perspective, one more determined thought remains: *babies shouldn't die.* And this thought is, in fact, just as biblical as the ones we've just described.

There are a myriad of ideas, theories, and assumptions around us as to what is wrong with the world, but everyone—

hristian and non-Christian—agrees that the world *isn't* as it should be. Babies shouldn't die. But where does the "should" come from?

In the apostle Paul's famous letter to the Romans, he makes some huge statements about the world's *brokenness*. He gives the Bible story in miniature: in the beginning, creation was very good (which is why we all have a "world as it should be" in our minds). Humans' rebellion against God caused a brokenness in ourselves and in the whole of creation. We are in "bondage to corruption"—that is why babies die, and that is *not* how life should be. But this brokenness is not here to stay.

> *The sufferings of this present time are not worth comparing with the glory that is to be revealed to us. For the creation waits with eager longing for the revealing of the sons of God. For the creation was subjected to futility, not willingly, but because of him who subjected it, in hope that the creation itself will be set free from its bondage to corruption and obtain the freedom of the glory of the children of God. (Romans 8 v 18-21)*

Notice that word "futility". Paul is deliberately quoting a hallmark word from Ecclesiastes, one of the books we quoted from earlier. Again and again Ecclesiastes says that life in this broken world is "vanity" (e.g. Ecclesiastes 1 v 2). It's a hard word to translate, rooted in the idea of a vapour that disappears and can't be held. We might say "transience" or "meaninglessness". Paul chooses "futility". (How do we know he has Ecclesiastes in mind? He uses the precise word which the Greek translation of the Hebrew Old Testament uses to translate the word in Ecclesiastes.)

Here then is our link: Job and Ecclesiastes confront the world's brokenness with honesty, and conclude that short lives are more blessed, since they pass more quickly through this evil age. Paul says something better. Through Jesus, this broken age will be "set free"— there will be a renewal of all creation. What is coming, for those who belong to God, is a wonderful, glorious future.

This gives us hope for our own little ones (see chapter 10 for more on this). And it gives us hope for ourselves. The sufferings of this present time are great indeed—but they are "not worth comparing with the glory that is to be revealed to us" (Romans 8 v 18). The world is not as it should be, but in Jesus we can have complete confidence that all things are going to be put right.

WHAT NOW?

We've seen that knowing and being known brings richness and meaning to a person's existence. This is just as true of us as it is of our little ones. If we will allow it to, our child's short life can therefore have the effect of *enriching* our subsequent earthly life.

We can never be the same now. Life will be irreversibly *richer* for having known our little one—however brief our experience of him or her was. Life will be richer, since every single moment and experience is connected in some way to the knowledge of our little one. For instance, each time we've been on holiday we've missed Jed, and wondered what holidays with him would have been like. We give thanks for him. When we and our children encounter sick or disabled children, we have a depth of sympathy for them and their families which we otherwise would not have had. Our children are far more invested in heaven than they would otherwise have been, since their brother has gone before them and they keenly await seeing him again.

You don't need to be a Christian to experience the truth of the saying "It's better to have loved and lost than never to have loved at all." To have loved and lost is better, since it enriches us. We move forward with a bigger heart.

We must choose thankfulness. Notice that the difference between thankfulness and resentment is always one of perspective. When we focus on what we have, we are thankful; when we focus on what we don't have, we are resentful. This is why enormously wealthy people can be bitterly preoccupied with not having more. And why very poor people can be buoyantly cheerful.

Choices confront us: Will we resent the shortness of our time with our little one here and now, or rejoice in the days we did have with them (even if that was just in the womb)? Will we resent the way grief has changed us, or choose to rejoice in the way God is shaping us to look forward more deeply to the coming age?

This is surely part of what the writer of Ecclesiastes means when he urges us at various points to enjoy "life under the sun" (e.g. Ecclesiastes 5 v 18; 9 v 9). To *choose thankfulness*, which is the same as choosing joy.

We are constantly thankful for the unshakeable hope we have in Jesus. We wish, on the one hand, that we could have seen Jed develop, play with his siblings, and become fully grown-up. We wish we could have got to know his character inside-out. But we are profoundly thankful, on the other hand, that Jed has been and is a part of our lives—that his life was not without meaning, that he has escaped the evil of this world, and that we can trust our good Lord with his future. We are thankful, too, to be confident that *we will know Jed*, we will get to know him inside-out, in the coming age (on which see chapter 10).

Dear friend, let the constant reminder of the little one you have lost turn you, above all, to the tender heart of God—the one who is "gentle and lowly in heart" (Matthew 11 v 28-29). Everything, for God's children, is a means of worship. There's an old hymn which says that, in comparison to knowing Jesus, the things of this earth "grow strangely dim". However, there's a real sense in which the things of this earth—including little lives that ended all too soon—can grow strangely *bright* as we see the Giver behind them. We are waiting for a better age; but we enjoy God's gifts and his creation here and now even within this broken world. And every life is a gift—short or long.

6. Past, Present, Future

For those facing the loss of an older child

by Chris Mouring

Our son Brian was 20 years old when he disappeared into the shallow ocean surf of a North Carolina beach. He was wrapping up a camping trip in August 2010 when he decided to take one last swim. Standing with a friend in waist-high water, Brian dove into a wave—and never resurfaced alive. In a single, inexplicable moment, he slipped beyond the frantic searching of his brother and friends and then of rescue boats and divers. Instantly, Brian's earthly history concluded, his earthly present disintegrated, and his earthly future evaporated. The resulting pain and trauma were beyond words.

It's an impossible task to say everything there is to say about losing an older child in a single short chapter. Fortunately, much of the rest of this book has help that is relevant for many different situations. But there is one thing that makes the loss of an older child unique, and this will be my focus here: the older the child, the more complex is that child's connection to their world. Their history is longer, their present is more intricate, their imagined future is more defined. Death's earth-shattering disruption of this past, present and future in turn disfigures the past, present and future of those left behind.

If you have lost a child, you already know that the path through such grief seems to be an impossible challenge. So much has been lost; death really does sting and the grave really does cry "Victory!" But in this chapter I want to show you that death and the grave do *not* have the last word; God does (1 Corinthians 15 v 55). Even now, there *is* hope!

INSEPARABLE LOVE

In our anguish over Brian, we sometimes wondered how we could even survive, let alone have hope, as we struggled to process our unspeakable loss. But even through our tears, hope *did* come, from our inseparable connection with our loving God and from many comforting biblical truths. In particular, much of Romans 8 greatly encouraged us. For example:

> *Who shall separate us from **the love of Christ**? Shall tribulation, or distress, or persecution, or famine, or nakedness, or danger, or sword? ... No, in all these things we are **more than conquerors** through him who loved us. For I am sure that neither death nor life, nor angels nor rulers, nor things present nor things to come, nor powers, nor height nor depth, nor anything else in all creation, will be able to separate us from **the love of God** in Christ Jesus our Lord. (Romans 8 v 35, 37-39)*

As Christians, *nothing*, not even the destabilizing death of a child, can separate us from the love of Christ or from the love of our heavenly Father. If we have put our trust in Jesus, we are permanently connected to a loving Savior who is powerful and present (Matthew 28 v 18, 20), compassionate and engaging (Mark 1 v 41), merciful and faithful (Hebrews 2 v 17), sympathetic and effective (Hebrews 4 v 15-16), and so much more. We are also permanently connected to a loving Father who is *for* us (Romans 8 v 31), *near* to the broken-hearted (Psalm 34 v 18), sovereign over *every* event in our lives (Job 1 v 21), and working *all* things together for our good (Romans 8 v 28). We have hope because we are connected to a loving, all-powerful God!

And not only can nothing separate us from the love of God, we also see that through Christ we *are*, right now, more than conquerors over *anything* that would try. *More* than conquerors, literally "super-conquerors". We have help and hope because—as we're going to see—whenever an enemy or roadblock attempts to hinder our faith or cause us to doubt the love of Jesus, that same glorious love can not only conquer it but make it serve our spiritual good. God does not magically erase our sorrow; we remain tattooed with grief. But in love he supernaturally repurposes it.

I don't know the specifics of your story, but I do know that because of Jesus, you, too, can be more than a conqueror— even as you struggle with your grief. There is *help* for processing a concluded history, a disintegrated present, an evaporated earthly future. There is *hope* amidst broken-heartedness over the loss of an older child.

A SHARED HISTORY

Because of our relatively long shared history together, Brian left many lingering traces. His fingerprints in our space include tangible touchstones like baby shoes and graduation certificates. His fingerprints on our hearts include fond memories—as my wife Kim wrote: "snuggly moments reading with him as a child, watching him laugh long and hard with his dad over a joke that only they thought was funny, hearing him call me 'mommy' even as a 20-year-old man". All around us and inside of us, Brian's absence is always present.

Those memories can prick like a needle because they cannot be repeated. Worse, regrets can stab like a knife because they cannot be recanted. I painfully remember many of my own actions or inactions that I wish I could revisit with Brian. With my living children, I can ask for forgiveness and improve the way I relate to them. Not so with Brian; what's done is done. Wrestling with these regrets added to the bitterness of my grief.

I am sure that you also could describe the impact on you and your family from the history you share with the child you have lost. You mourn the inability to repeat the good times. You grieve your mistakes. But both bittersweet memories and stinging regrets *can* be more than conquered. Look with me at another section in Romans 8:

> *And we know that for those who love God all things work together for good, for those who are called according to his purpose … What then shall we say to these things? If God is for us, who can be against us? He who did not spare his own Son but gave him up for us all, how will he not also with him graciously give us all things? Who shall bring any charge against God's elect? It is God who justifies. Who is to condemn? Christ Jesus is the one who died— more than that, who was raised—who is at the right hand of God, who indeed is interceding for us.*
>
> *(Romans 8 v 28, 31-34)*

God works *all* things together for good for his children. He is *for* us. And because God loved us enough to give up his Son for us, he will certainly give us all the things that he knows are best for us. These things together have a profound effect on how we process both our bittersweet memories and our painful regrets.

GOD'S GRACIOUS GIFTS

Memories embody blessing. Reflecting on my shared history with Brian, I can clearly see that I am a different man now than I would have been without him. I learned more about joy through his joy. I learned more about sorrow through his sorrow. My love for Brian expanded my heart and made me a more loving person. All that he was and did had a permanent impact on me. Memories, therefore, are a good gift from God. Rather than focusing on the fact that they cannot be repeated, I—and you—can focus on being thankful for the blessings they embody.

I am now thankful even for the painful regrets. Not so much for them in and of themselves, but for what God has taught me through them. We can see in the final part of the passage above that in Jesus, our sinful mistakes are forgiven; they cannot condemn us. Therefore, when our regrets reproach us, we can take them to Jesus, ask for his forgiveness, wisely learn from them, and *not* be oppressed or crippled by them. This channels our regrets, like our memories, to also serve our good.

Do you see? God enables us to be more than conquerors as we start to see our shared history with our child as a gift. The Brian-shaped hole in my life remains, and I will never stop missing him this side of heaven. But the memories are treasured and even the regrets begin to help me more than they hurt. Rather than *separate* me from God's love, my history with Brian *shows* me God's love.

I am sure there are many ways in which you have been blessed by the history you share with the child you have lost. In your grief, can you embrace those good memories and be thankful for how they have impacted you? I'm also confident there are many lessons you have learned from the mistakes you made. In your grief, can you address your regrets, learn from them, and release them to the gracious forgiveness of God in Jesus? Can you allow God to sanctify and bless your past—painful though it might feel at the moment?

In all things give thanks, even in your grief-tinged "new normal". You can be thankful for the shared history you have with your child. You can be more than a conqueror because of Jesus' love.

AN INTRICATE PRESENT

Brian's death not only flooded us with a torrent of emotional trauma, it also unleashed a massive earthquake within the logistics of our everyday lives. Everything routine stopped and the surreal interaction with the business side of death, like picking out his coffin and writing his obituary, began immediately. And because Brian was 20, his life had many complex details; he had a job, he owned a car, he was a college student. Kim and I had to address much of this while still under the confusing and distracting pall of loss.

Then there were the many relationships impacted by Brian's death. In addition to the connections that Kim and I had with Brian's grandparents, his siblings, and our extended family, there were also his teachers, his sports coaches, the parents of his friends, our neighbors, our fellow church members, and many others. When Brian died, we not only carried our own grief but also shared in the grief of many other mourners.

I expect you could tell the story of how your own grief has been complicated by disrupted logistics and destabilized relationships. In this fractured present, and when we are fractured ourselves, how can we be "more than conquerors"?

An important approach for us was to let God's character and promises shed divine light on our grief. In our shattered moments, you and I must rely on our solid, inseparable connection to a loving God—a heavenly Father who is both good and great. This enables us to see our heavy logistics and hurting relationships in a different light.

GOOD AS WELL AS GREAT

The Bible is clear about the *greatness* of God: he is in complete control of everything that happens in our lives. Jesus says he has all authority in heaven and on earth (Matthew 28 v 18). This means that God had the power to *not* take Brian. Jesus had the authority to save him from the waves.

The Bible is also clear about the *goodness* of God. We have already seen that God is for us (Romans 8 v 31), that he is working all things for our good (v 28), and that nothing can separate us from his love (v 39). This leads to a gnawing question: "Why, God?" How can we reconcile God's greatness with his goodness—his decision to take our child and his promise to love us and work all things for our good?

Part of answering that question is to realize that God's goodness is not at odds with his greatness. In fact, God's greatness is demonstrated in the fact that he is able to work all things—even bad things—for our good. God's great power is what enables him to be truly, fully good.

To begin with, you might not see what good God could possibly be working through what has happened. It's often only later that it becomes clearer. For us, over a period of years, God has allowed us to see much good stemming from Brian's death: in particular, the salvation of souls and spiritual growth in ourselves and others. We have seen spiritual beauty rising from the ashes of death, and that has confirmed our trust in God's loving goodness and greatness—making us more than conquerors in a horrific situation that could have easily crippled our faith.

But even at the very start of the grief journey, there is comfort and rest to be found in the truths that God is both great and good. God was not absent, sleeping, or apathetic as Brian's life ended under the waves. Nor was he when your child left this life. Nor is he now.

GOODNESS IN GRIEF

The night Brian disappeared in the ocean, Kim and I gathered with our immediate family and a few close friends not far from where he had vanished (it was the following day that his body washed up on shore about a mile away). The first thing we did was pray and share our grief with our Savior, and ask for his strength and wisdom to "grieve well" to the glory of God. We did not know yet what that would look like but we knew for sure that we needed help, that we needed to rest firmly in God's goodness and greatness and on the power and presence of Jesus.

That night we decided as a family to grieve publicly and honestly. Not everyone needs to or should grieve completely or even partly in public, of course. But in our situation, with so many co-grievers, we felt led to provide raw insight into what it means to grieve as Christians. Many among our family and friends were hurting and questioning. Many were subconsciously watching us for clues about how to process their own grief. We didn't know how to proceed or what we would face—but we felt it was our responsibility to honestly examine the jagged intersection of our faith and our grief and to share our real-time learning curve with others.

We were disoriented and overwhelmed at times, but we knew that God was great and good. Our perspective was increasingly one of patience and trust in his plan. We did not know all the "how" but we did know the "why". God was promoting our good and his glory and we kept that clear in our minds, even as much else was fuzzy. The complex logistics did not ultimately separate us from our loving God but instead drove us straight to him: straight to his mercy and grace and his surpassing power (helpful passages at the time included Hebrews 4 v 16; Philippians 4 v 11-13; 2 Corinthians 4 v 7; 12 v 9). When we could not stand, we fell on Jesus. Then, over time, it felt as if he enabled us by his Spirit to start to run on crippled legs, to fly with broken wings.

This was how God brought good out of our situation—not only for us, but for many others. Many people wanted to know how it was possible for us to reconcile the hideous process of grieving Brian's death with our steadfast confidence in God. As we grieved openly and tried to distill our grief and faith into words, the wide community responded. We were able to "vent" our grief, others were able to learn from us, and God used the whole process to clarify our reliance on him and to deepen our relationship with Jesus—and to bring some others to faith for the first time.

This is what it looked like for us to process our grief over Brian's interrupted intricate present. We leaned hard on God's goodness and greatness and on the power and presence of Jesus to give us patience and perspective. God empowered us to more than conquer the challenges we faced from the "abnormal" logistics of death and the widespread community grief. God grew us spiritually in and with our broken present.

In your own crippling grief, it may feel like trusting in our good and great God is almost impossible. But resting in the power and presence of Jesus is the only way to deal with your own disrupted present. Ask him for help; in Jesus, nothing can separate you from God's love, not even death. You will be more than a conqueror as you take your painful present to Jesus right now and trust him with your eternity.

AN IMAGINED FUTURE

When he died, Brian was studying to be a civil engineer; I was looking forward to the day when he would be a peer in the world of work. That expectation for him vanished, along with so many others. Coming to terms with the loss of our hopes and dreams for our children's future—dreams which have taken increasingly solid shape as they have grown—is an inescapable, awful part of grieving.

It wasn't just Brian's future we had lost; it was our own future, with him. He would no longer be a part of our holiday celebrations, future weddings, or family vacations. He would no longer participate in mundane time together doing routine activities—a loss that now seems neither mundane nor routine. As we navigated our *new* earthly future, it felt like Brian was a buoy fixed in the river of time as the rest of us drifted further and further away from him. The earthly future we had all imagined was gone forever. But I have purposefully

been using the qualifier "earthly" in front of "future". Let's
look at two more verses of Romans 8:

> *For I consider that the sufferings of this present time are*
> *not worth comparing with the glory that is to be revealed*
> *to us. For the creation waits with eager longing for the*
> *revealing of the sons of God. (Romans 8 v 18-19)*

Since there is both a "present" time and a "to be" time, one
thing these two verses teach us is that there is more to life than
just the here and now. And we see that the suffering of this
earthly "present" time will be massively eclipsed by the glory of
the heavenly "to be" time. We are also reminded that not even
death can separate the child of God from the love of Christ.

Understanding the distinction between our earthly future
and our heavenly future was the main truth that helped Kim
and I process the "lost earthly future" component of our grief.
Earthly death is without a doubt grievous, traumatic, and
horrible, but it is ultimately a pretender. Jesus has defeated
death and the grave, and their days are numbered. Even now,
death ultimately serves the good of every believer.

Brian professed faith in Jesus Christ just 3 months before
he died, so he is only temporarily separated from us. Though
temporary, this forced separation is nonetheless horrendous;
my daughter Rachel, who lost her own 3-year-old son, calls
it the "nearly unbearable intermission". But because of our
shared hope in the person and saving work of Jesus, we know
our futures are destined to reconverge.

Yet as great as the reunion with Brian will be, it is not the
main blessing of eternal life in heaven. In fact, seeing our loved
ones in heaven is not even mentioned by Paul in Romans 8.
This is an important observation for those of us who are

unsure of our children's spiritual state. It shifts the focus from our uncertainty around who will be with us in heaven to the certainty of our eternal enjoyment of the glorious and inseparable love of Jesus. We can leave our uncertainty at throne of God. As Dan and Anna write in chapter 10, "We can trust that God, the judge of all the earth, will 'do what is right' (Genesis 18 v 25)."

Our focus in eternity will be on Jesus; the greatest thing about experiencing heaven will be experiencing him. We will see our Savior face to face and be with him forever, We will experience his inseparable love in a sinless state, and because of that love, we will obtain ultimate "more than a conqueror" status for all eternity. The "to be" time outweighs even the greatest sufferings and separations of the "present" time, because, hard though it may be to realize it now, the glory of Christ more than conquers the sting of death. As he slipped under the waves and beyond our reach, Brian more than conquered death because it carried him straight to his heavenly future and into the arms of Jesus. *We, too,* are more than conquerors over death as we hope in something, someONE bigger than death. Jesus is the foundational, central, and overarching joy of heaven, and the joy of Jesus will intensify our experience of all the other joys of heaven as well. Anticipating this is the greatest comfort I can think of in a difficult present.

MORE THAN CONQUERORS

If there's one thing you take away from this chapter, I hope it is a sense of how critical our inseparable connection with our loving God is. Through the power, presence, and promises of Jesus, we are more than conquerors over the pain and trauma of grief. I cannot overemphasize the tremendous help and hope Kim and I have experienced in those truths.

I know this chapter has certainly *not* answered every painful question or addressed every traumatic situation. To be clear, it would be a mistake to minimize grief in some sort of quasi-spiritual, Pollyanna way. Death is a terrible consuming monster. But as we grasp its pervasive horror, we also more fully appreciate its ultimate defeat. As we have seen in this chapter, and as you know by experience, our faith is not some sort of heavenly white-out that blots the ink of searing loss from the story of our lives. Rather, in the spirit of super-conquering, our faith points us to the loving Author of our story who enables us to recast the paragraphs of pain as stories of bitter blessings and incognito graces. When sanctified by God, our darkest distresses yoke us to him more firmly and fit us for service to others by enlarging our hearts and giving us wisdom forged in the fire of stark reality. Our struggles give us more of God himself. We do not have all the answers, but we know the one who does.

Our son Brian is gone from this life. Period. We feel it keenly. It is incomprehensible, the effects are devastating. Grief stains, grief stings, grief stays; it is obnoxious and incredibly frustrating. And yet, losing Brian has also been an astounding journey, with much good and many Christ-exalting events and implications. Kim and I still grieve deeply, and will until we die—but not as those who have no hope.

7. Valuable

For those facing the possibility that their

child will be disabled

This chapter is for all those who need clarity or reassurance about the value of their child's life. In a way this might seem a surprising chapter to feature in a book about the loss of a child. Nevertheless, we write this because facing the possibility of losing your child can often also involve facing the alternative possibility of your child living with severe disabilities.

If you listen to some parts of our culture, having a child with severe disabilities is tantamount to losing them. When Anna was pregnant with Jed, we were given the option of a "selective termination"; an injection into the womb to end Jed's life (which incidentally came with a significant risk to Ethan, his identical twin, who was healthy). The reason we were offered this was, "You have to think about Jed's *quality of life*, and the *burden* that it will be on your family as well". The tacit message was: if Jed lives, it will be with enormous health problems, and life will be so awful that he might as well be dead.

We don't know your story. Perhaps your child has had a terrible accident; whilst there is hope that they will survive, you fear the extra needs they will have if they do. Perhaps you are in a situation more like ours with Jed, looking out onto a future which holds either death or severe disability for your child after their birth—with pressure on you to choose. Perhaps you are well past that initial storm with your own child, and need reassurance that you made the right choice.

We can't give specific advice into every situation. In particular, Jed didn't live, and so we can't speak with authority into the experience of actually caring for a severely disabled child. Nevertheless, we can reassure you of the *value* of your child's life—every child's life. This, we hope, can be a stable foundation for you as you navigate the difficult decisions and experiences that are to come.

A GOD WHO CARES

If you read the Bible, it's hard to miss the fact that God cares for disabled people: they are given dignity throughout the Scriptures. We might think of King David's care for Mephibosheth, a disabled man (2 Samuel 9), or the numerous accounts of Jesus' care for sick, blind, crippled, deaf and mute people. There are occasions where people actively try to stop socially unwanted, disabled people from getting near to Jesus, but his compassion is unstoppable (e.g. Matthew 20 v 29-34). It is the same with the very youngest and smallest people (e.g. Mark 10 v 13-14). So, if you fear the layer upon layer of physical and social difficulty that your child may face, you can be confident that God knows your fears, and disability does not take him by surprise. He sees your situation and is with you in it.

All people, everywhere, however young or old, wanted or unwanted, abled or disabled, are worthy of dignity, care and protection, simply because they are people. Sadly, this is not always the attitude of the society we live in. So what we are going to do next is to examine two of the main ways in which our culture often talks about the value of people, and see why each falls short.

FUNCTION

Some may think that life is valuable because of its *function*—in other words, what a person is *capable of doing*. Some may think that a life is not worth living if a person can't walk or talk, or manage basic self-care. Some may think that greater intellectual or physical abilities, or greater earning-power, or social skill, makes a person more valuable.

This way of thinking falls apart when you scrutinise it, since function varies through our lifetime. To be consistent with this view we'd need to say we're not valuable as babies and children, then we become more valuable as adults (unless we suffer unemployment, or a dark season of mental-health struggles, or chronic illness, or a disability), and then we decline in value again in older age. This is a very unstable way to value life.

Most people wouldn't explicitly say that a child isn't valuable because they can't (and perhaps won't ever be able to) dress or feed themselves. But this idea—that value is tied to function—does underlie some of the ways people talk about whether to, for example, end an unborn child's life.

QUALITY OF LIFE

Take the phrase *quality of life*. People might reason, "If a child could never walk or talk or wash themselves, their quality of life would be terrible and so it would be better for them not to live." The implicit assumption is that *function and quality of life are the same thing.* But they are not. You and I simply do not have the right to presume that we know what another's quality of life is or would be. We certainly have no right to presume that quality of life is lower because someone is less functional. For instance, think about the happiest people you know. Are they the highest achievers, the most "functional" ones? Think about the people with disabilities you know. Are they wallowing in desperate despair, unlike all the super-achievers out there? No. Happiness and quality of life do not rest on being able to do everything.

In fact, the Bible actually dignifies weakness in an utterly radical way. The logic of Jesus' kingdom is consistently "upside-down" by comparison with the world's assumptions. The last shall be first (Matthew 20 v 16); God dwells with the one who is lowly in spirit (Isaiah 57 v 15); God has chosen the despised things of this world (1 Corinthians 1 v 28); God's power is made perfect in weakness (2 Corinthians 12 v 9); and above all it is through Jesus' self-giving, shameful death that God saves. This is why Paul says that he boasts in his weaknesses (2 Corinthians 12 v 9): since he is so confident that God works most clearly through our *inabilities.* In other words, our *lack* of function.

Had Jed lived, we are confident that he would have known a quality of life that eludes very many. He had a loving mum and dad, siblings who loved him to bits, and a loving and supportive church family. *Quality of life is linked to mutual love,* not to function. To be known and loved by people—really, loyally, known and loved—is what gives an unshakeable quality of life. Above all, to bask in the warm knowledge of God the Father's love for us through Jesus his Son. It's a mirage to think that quality of life comes from what you can do for yourself. It is lazy thinking to say, "Because a child has (or will have) extra needs they must be unhappy."

Please don't misunderstand us. Life with a child with severe disabilities is full of pains, stresses, disappointments and profound limitations. Many of the struggles that parents of children with disabilities have to navigate are completely beyond the awareness of other parents. If your child has had disabilities diagnosed, then peering into the future is understandably terrifying. We are in no way dismissing this. The point we are making here is simply that we cannot base quality of life on function. Nor, even if quality of life is indeed low, can we decide that a life is less valuable on that basis— because quality of life changes.

The ultimate quality of life is to know and enjoy God for ever, and that is possible even amid the greatest pain. Since you are reading this book, it is likely that you and your family are experiencing unwanted limits, griefs, and weaknesses. Can you see that, through Jesus, our lack of function—our disabilities, our limits, our failures, our burdens—don't in any way keep us from him?

WANTEDNESS
Then there's *wantedness*. This concept is often used to talk about pregnancies. But if we don't want a baby at a particular time, is that a legitimate way of declaring an unborn child to have less worth? If we heard that an orphaned street girl in a deprived community, who was not loved or wanted by anyone, had been trafficked and abused, we would be (quite rightly) outraged, since we know she is still worthy of care, dignity, protection and nurture. Who would dare disagree

with that statement? Now make her a few years younger, and unborn. What's the moral difference?

This is not to say that there is not a tremendous complexity and need for help and support for women who find themselves pregnant in a season in life where they cannot bear the thought of a future with a baby. This is no simple thing. And help is out there (please see Appendix II for more details). But we want to insist that the pain and chaos of this situation will not be solved or removed by *removing a person*.

In addition, wantedness (like function) varies massively. An unwanted street child might grow up to become a dad, a nurse, a charity worker in the same slums; someone dearly loved and relied upon by many. There are countless examples of people with such life-stories. Would anyone say to them, "It would have been better if your life had ended in infancy when you were unwanted"?

Above all we must ask, "unwanted by whom?" The God of the Bible is clear that he cares sincerely and steadily for disabled people and socially "unwanted" people. They are wanted by him. And if this is true, what right do we have to treat any human as unwanted?

This is the ground for your *courage* as a parent as you look to the future. You are not condemned for feeling, "I don't want a disabled child!" Instead, the fact that God has given you a child with extra needs is an implicit pledge that he will give you grace for each step of the way ahead, as you lean upon him. His care is the foundation, not yours. He knows your needs, he knows your fears. Are you prepared to trust him, one step at a time?

MADE IN GOD'S IMAGE

How can we be so certain that God is concerned for all humans, however sick or disabled? In the very first chapter of the Bible we meet a vitally important phrase. In some ways it's a cryptic one: God made humans "in his own image" (Genesis 1 v 26-27). What does this mean? People have suggested all kinds of answers, often based on the idea that humans are able to *do* things which animals can't, such as make moral decisions, or perform certain creative activities. But this is just another form of linking value to function—and it is not what the Bible actually says.

Genesis isn't saying there is something that humans *do* which shows they are in the image of God. Rather, it is saying that to be human is already to *exist in relation to God*; to exist on planet Earth as God's image-bearer. It's perfectly legitimate to say something like, "Since we're made in the image of God, we naturally find ways to communicate and be creative." But we must never get that backwards: we cannot say, "Finding ways to communicate and be creative is what imaging God is all about, and thus what makes us human."

To be human is to be in the image of God: to represent God on planet Earth, to be like him, *simply by virtue of being human.* It's not that by being or doing something you fulfil the image of God. It's that by being human, you are already in the image of God. Humanness is image-of-God-ness. And since we are in the image of God, all humans are inherently precious.

We thus have a clear and solid place from which to make decisions about human life. Human life is immeasurably, inherently, valuable, *because it is in the image of God.* All people, everywhere, however young or old, wanted or unwanted, abled or disabled, are worthy of dignity, care, and protection simply because they are people—because they bear God's image.

This is a firm anchor in our turmoil: your child is immeasurably precious to God, because he or she is in his image. Caring, protecting, honouring, advocating for and serving your child is something dear to God's heart. He is with you on this journey.

WHEN DOES LIFE BEGIN?

Our first question—"what gives life value?"—is directly related to a second: "when does life begin?" This is of particular importance to those who are pregnant and seeking wisdom about the way forward. Some may feel pressured to end a baby's life not because they doubt the inherent value of human life but because they are not convinced that their unborn child is fully human yet. So the question really matters: when does life begin?

Some suggest that life begins at a certain stage of gestation, like 24 weeks old, when an unborn child is *legally* deemed to be a person (in the UK; the figure differs elsewhere). This age was originally based on the capabilities of medical technology: babies born before 24 weeks were unlikely to survive. Therefore, this argument goes, it's morally acceptable to end the life of an unborn child before 24 weeks. Do you see how this is a "function" perspective? Life is deemed to begin when a baby is functionally able to live outside the womb, with medical support. But logically, this view has to revise itself periodically to keep up with medical advances, shifting the age when life "begins" earlier and earlier. It's hardly stable ground.

Some people say that life begins when the heartbeat can

be picked up at a scan. This is also a "function" argument, since it is rooted in our ability to assess something that the person's body can *do*. If someone has a heart attack and their heart stops beating for a couple of minutes before paramedics manage to restart it, did they stop being a person for those two minutes? This argument is, again, also linked to the shifting ground of technology. An old ultrasound scanner may not pick up the heartbeat that a more modern machine would. Is this a solid way to ascribe value to life?

On top of all this, the developmental age when the heart starts to beat, accepted as six weeks' gestation, is not some magic moment when a switch gets turned on and the heart "starts". Rather, tiny babies at first don't *need* a pump, since their bodies are so small; they first have a central tube which supplies blood to the growing baby. This tube seamlessly develops into a heart, and the flow of blood within it gradually takes on an eventually discernible beat. There is no "magic moment".

Another suggestion is that life begins when pain can be experienced. We find similar problems here too. If someone has an anaesthetic for an operation and doesn't experience pain for a while, they don't stop being a person during that time. What this argument actually means is that a baby becomes a person when their experience of pain can be *measured*; when particular responses to painful stimuli can be observed. The big assumption here is that we know precisely what we're looking for and can measure it. What if we don't, and we can't?

Logically, then, there's only one sure way to answer the question "when does life begin?" Answer: it begins at the very beginning, at conception, when genetic material from the mother and father fuse in a unique way to create a brand-new human life.

This is the Bible's position. Consider David, who wrote that God had "known" him and "knitted [him] together" in the womb as an unborn baby; and even—spectacularly—that God "saw [his] unformed substance" (Psalm 139 v 16). Luke refers to the unborn John the Baptist with the same Greek word, *brephos*, that he uses elsewhere for an infant (Luke 1 v 44; 2 v 16). Unborn or born, you're a person in the Bible's eyes.

All of this means that if we are asked a question like "Do you want to continue with this pregnancy?" we can, through tears, most unashamedly say *yes*. Abortion—except sometimes in rare cases where the physical life of the mother is in grave danger—is not the answer. As soon as we come to realise that a tiny baby is fully a person from conception, we can see that we do not have the moral right to harm him or her.

Sadly, many parents find themselves coming under pressure to end the life of their baby. This pressure may come from friends or family or from medical professionals. As we have already seen, it is often put in plausible and well-meaning terms: "You have to think about what their quality of life will be... Think of the suffering... Think of your own quality of life." We have tried to show that these statements do not withstand scrutiny. A person's value does not come from their level of function, nor from their quality of life, nor from their wantedness. Medics can make judgements as to whether a *treatment* is not worth *giving*. None of us can say that a *life* is not worth *living*.

We know that there are many more questions some readers may have about this whole issue. We'd highly recommend *Matters of Life and Death* by John Wyatt.

Before we continue: we know that for some readers, this chapter may bring back painful memories of situations where the choices you made or were pressured into contributed to a little life ending. We can only say: *come to Jesus.* How much kindness and forgiveness is there for you? As much as you need. And not only forgiveness, but full and complete redemption. Trust that our Father God is able—somehow, in the fullness of time—to bring about beauty from brokenness. He is unstoppable. How can we be sure? Jesus was once crucified, but now he lives for ever.

PRESSING ON WITH COURAGE

What if you *are* prepared to go through with this pregnancy, but nevertheless feel utterly terrified, utterly bleak about the future? Or what if right now you find yourself at a point of complete despair over the difficulties your child is facing? We wish we could be with you face to face, to put an arm on your shoulder and tell you of the utmost respect we have for your courage. Here is what we know for sure.

First, *no matter how short a time you have with them, you can choose to savour your little one's life.* We wrote more about this in chapter 5. The time you have with your child—short or long—is a gift. Even though disease or disability threatens to shorten their life, will you focus more on the time you do have than on the time you might not? For those who are still pregnant: in the midst of all the unknowns, will you look ahead to their birth as a *gift*? You will hold them, see them, enjoy them, love them. This season of your life is an unrepeatable opportunity. To reassure those carrying similar concerns, Anna had lurking fears that Jed's deformities might make it harder for her to love him; in fact, the brokenness of his body only increased the tenderness of our love and compassion for him.

Second, *you shouldn't assume you know how this will unfold.* We don't know the facts of your situation, your past journey, or how complicated and threatening your future looks. But God does. Trust God for the future. Don't assume you know how this will unfold. No one has the power to predict the future. But God is always a refuge for those who trust in him. Every time the fear of the future comes knocking at the door, you can roll that thought to God's mighty shoulders. Try using the word "but": "I am absolutely dreading what my life is going to look like *but* God is in control, and he is good, and I will trust him" (for more on this, see the postscript to chapter 1). When we were faced with the terrifying prospect of giving birth to a very ill little boy, and then watching him die, Anna understood the fear which causes some women to opt for medical termination. The prospect seemed unbearable. But God's promises proved true yet again; his grace transformed the dark valley into something beautiful.

Third, *it is a beautiful thing to serve and suffer for those who are dishonoured and overlooked by the world.* Some parents will know the appalling, gut-wrenching feeling when others imply that it would have been better if their child had not been born. Others will know the quiet, often lonely, always ongoing, cost of raising and caring for a child with ill health or disabilities. If you are a follower of Jesus, then all your limits, losses, shames and sufferings of this life will—somehow—translate into glory in the life to come (e.g. Psalm 126 v 5-6). Please will you rest in that? A great reversal is coming, guaranteed by the resurrection of Jesus. Even if you are overlooked by everyone else, our Father in heaven sees—just as he saw our "unformed substance" when no one else knew us (Psalm 139 v 16). It is a beautiful thing to serve and suffer for those who are dishonoured by the world.

As we conclude this chapter, we want to revisit our core question and find a final note of comfort within it. What gives *you* value? We've asked this with little people in mind, but what about you and me? Does our value come from how wise and able we are as parents? From how healthily babies could grow within our own bodies? From how many children we have, and how healthy and happy they are? From how in control we are of our situations? No, no, no, and no. You and I have been valuable since the moment we began to exist as a unique person, there at conception, unseen to others but known and intended by God. At the end of the day then, we aren't the final author of our own lives—he is. We no longer need to despair at these problems we cannot solve. We need to turn to him in trust; we are in his image, and we will find our humanness and our rest in him.

8. Walking Together

For family and friends

This chapter is for those who walk alongside grieving parents. You might be their friends, members of their church, their pastors, or their family. *Whoever you are, thank you* for being prepared to find a way to care for them through this. We were loved and blessed by our church, family and friends during the year that we carried and lost Jed, and ever since, in far more ways than we can ever count or express.

Grieving parents are suffering in many ways at once. Their most obvious pain is the raw emotional trauma relating to the loss of their child. Often they will also be carrying the emotional burden of concern for others; for their spouse, and their other children if they have them. It is very likely that they will also experience some kind of significant financial or practical pressure in this season. Have they needed to stop working at some point through all of this? If they have other children to care for, are they balancing school runs and hospital trips? They may be haunted by questions in the background like "How am I going to manage?" They may be grappling with weighty questions of faith.

Significant suffering often goes hand in hand with relational isolation, as it becomes harder to be in social settings—either through necessity (e.g. hospital appointments) or preference (e.g. finding it hard to be around lots of happy people). Just the effort of grasping for words to describe how you are doing is tiring. Sometimes people have been especially bruised by insensitive comments from others, which further reduces their capacity to want to see people. Parenting may be more of a struggle. We found that at times there was a double-whammy of understandably challenging behaviour from our girls (because of their own grief and the uncertainty of the season) and reduced parenting abilities from us (because of our grief). The Lord's grace carried us through, but there were many times our home wasn't a beautiful place.

For some parents, they may also be carrying some form of physical pain in their own bodies. Perhaps they are postnatal mothers. Perhaps their health has deteriorated through the sustained stress of this season. Perhaps the needs of their sick child meant that their own health needs have been put on the backburner. Grieving parents are suffering in many ways at once, most of them probably unseen and difficult to help with. So once again, *thank you for walking alongside them*. This is no small thing.

In this chapter we will first of all consider *what enables us* to walk together. Then we will consider *what* it actually entails, and finally some specifics for *how* to walk alongside those who have lost, or face the prospect of losing, a child.

EMPOWERED TO LOVE
The best way for us to begin to work out how we are going to love those suffering is to look to Jesus. In him we will find we

have the energising power for persevering Christian love. We love "because he first loved us" (1 John 4 v 19). In other words, Christians are to trace out the ways of Jesus in gentle, patient, costly love of others. We draw strength to love others from the love Jesus shows us. This alone is literally a lifetime's work. But there's more.

A core theme of the New Testament is that Jesus is united to his people, and they are united to him. The metaphor of a body is used more than once (Romans 12 v 4-5; 1 Corinthians 12 v 12-27); Jesus is the head, and we are "members" of his body. In other words, to be a follower of Jesus is to be organically connected to him, to have been "incorporated" into him. This is a radically different concept to a gym membership, or an online video-streaming membership. Those are impersonal transactions which you can cancel anytime. By contrast, being a *member of Christ's body* means that Jesus is one with his people, and thus all that is his is ours. Theologians call this "union with Christ". It is why, when you read the New Testament, you keep noticing the little phrase "in Christ".

And if we are members of Jesus, we are therefore *members of one another*, just like your big toe and your left ear belong to each other since they are members of the same body. This is the realisation that makes all the difference. We don't love one another simply because it makes the world a better place, or because it's what good Christians do. We love other Christians because we ourselves are organically connected to them in the Lord Jesus. *We show our love for Jesus through our love for one another* (John 13 v 35).

A related concept which crops up in the New Testament is that of "fellowship". The original Greek word is also sometimes translated as community, participation or partnership. It's a real-life, earthy word. For instance, when we meet Peter the disciple in Luke 5, we're told that he had a fishing *partnership* with James and John. We can understand this: all three were fishermen, but they weren't in competition with each other; they were *partners*. One goes to the other's boat to help him with a net full of fish. They share the struggles and share the joy. That same word is used repeatedly to describe our relationship with Jesus and one another: partnership, participation, fellowship. For instance, the apostle John wrote to early churches describing himself as "your brother and *partner* in the tribulation and the kingdom and the patient endurance that are in Jesus" (Revelation 1 v 9). Paul writes that we have a "*participation* in his [Jesus'] sufferings" (Philippians 3 v 10 NIV). When we realise this, it is inevitable that as fellow Christians we share our joys—and share our struggles.

Finally, this underlying reality of being "in Christ" together is what drives the Bible's commands and invitations to demonstrate things like forgiveness, patience with one another, and brotherly love. Since we are fundamentally connected to one another, our love must have a deep and unbreakable "sibling" loyalty to it. If I am in Christ, and you are in Christ, then we are members of each other. We are partners. Your pain is my pain. Your joy gives me joy. My love *from* Jesus flows as my love *for* you. His love for you flows in part through me.

So we look to Jesus, asking for his help, and find ourselves empowered to love. In him, we are his hands and feet; we are partners, brothers, sisters of those who suffer. We love because he first loved us.

WHAT DOES LOVE LOOK LIKE?

With all that in mind, here are some of the Bible's specific commands for loving brothers and sisters who are in the midst of hard things.

> *Bear one another's burdens, and so fulfil the law of Christ.*
> *(Galatians 6 v 2)*

Note this: helping real people with real-world problems in real time is how you "fulfil" the law of Christ. Living as a Jesus-follower is not an abstract idea merely to be discussed. It is to be shown, embodied, fulfilled in real time through our acts of love involving particular people, places, words, actions and times.

Perhaps you know the story Jesus told about the "good Samaritan" (Luke 10 v 25-37). In this famous parable, a lone traveller is attacked and left for dead on the road. Two religious leaders, also travelling that road, each pass him by. But a third passer-by, a Samaritan—Samaritans and Jews hated each other—stops and cares for the wounded man. He takes him to an inn, provides medical attention, and foots all the bills.

The reason to mention the parable here is that it fleshes out Galatians 6 v 2. In fact, Jesus tells the parable precisely because he has been asked questions about how you obey God's law. The parable shows that obedience to God is not so much about formal religious activity as it is about a willingness to accept, in real time, the unwanted, messy and costly opportunities to love a specific human being. Obedience to Jesus consists not only of things *we choose* to do with our lives, but of accepting and embracing the cost of helping others in situations *we really didn't want or choose.*

Perhaps you are reading this chapter with a sinking feeling in your heart about the coming months and years. If you are honest, this sinking feeling is not entirely about the sadness of a death of a child for your friend or family member. It is in part a sinking feeling about the impact this is going to have on you, if you fully commit to walking with them through this. Please know this: it is a beautiful thing in the Lord's sight to spend yourself so that others can be refreshed. It is what Jesus himself did for us. Bear one another's burdens and in this way fulfil the law of Christ. Jesus "underwrites" his people as they love. Lean upon him and he will bear your burdens, as you bear the burdens of others (see Psalm 68 v 19; Matthew 11 v 28; 1 Peter 5 v 7).

> *Let love be genuine ... Love one another with brotherly affection ... Contribute to the needs of the saints ... weep with those who weep. (Romans 12 v 9-15)*

In this passage we find three important details or angles. Firstly, that we're to love with brotherly affection. As we thought about above, Christian love is love which flows out of an existing family relationship. Through Jesus we are children of God, and therefore brothers and sisters of one another. Thus, "brotherly" love is a "through thick and thin", long-term, loyal love. It's this kind of committed love for one another which is so hard to come by, even in churches. Let us keep going with Jesus-empowered brotherly love.

Then there's contributing to the needs of the saints. "Saint" in the Bible is originally a word which applies to all Christians, meaning "a set-apart one". If you're a Christian then you have, through Jesus, been brought near to God as his child, his treasured possession, his set-apart one, his *saint.*

And since we've been *set apart together in Jesus*, we treat each other in this way. This includes meeting one another's needs. We'll return to this more practically below.

Finally, weep with those who weep. This means what it says. There's a precious place for wise and thoughtful counselling, for gentle rebuke, for passionate encouragement, for teaching, for singing. But there is also a place for simply weeping. We are prone to overlook this as it feels unproductive. Some of us dislike the very idea since it feels like wallowing in negative emotions. But what does "productive" even look like after a major grief? Maybe we won't cry literal tears. What this phrase has in mind is the willingness to enter into the experience, to share it and feel it. It may simply look like long periods of silence together.

Be patient with them all. (1 Thessalonians 5 v 14)

One more verse before we get more practical. Towards the end of his letter to the Thessalonian church, the apostle Paul gives a rapid sequence of instructions for how to love one another (1 Thessalonians 5 v 12-28). They are simple yet profoundly wise, giving the core of how to help people in different kinds of struggles and situations. After the instructions he simply concludes, "Be patient with them all". It's the kind of phrase that gets overlooked. Yet it always applies. Maybe some in the church are persisting lazily in sin; maybe some are struggling ever to be encouraged. The overarching message is, *be patient with all of them*. Please bear this in mind as you walk alongside your grieving brothers and sisters. The Lord Jesus calls you, invites you, to be a channel for his love. And his love is a patient, gentle love.

People who have been through hard things rarely meet any

kind of schedule of recovery. As we've considered elsewhere in the book, recovery itself is a mirage. We should think more of a total reorganisation of life. Your grieving friends may have a really bad patch, two years on. They may still struggle to make decisions about little things. Whatever else you do, make sure you are walking in patience with them.

HOW?

For the remainder of this chapter, with the above verses in mind, we'll make practical suggestions. Here's one thing to note about them all: they are all costly in some way. Real love and care comes *at a cost*. It takes time, it takes decisions and headspace, it takes lots of messaging, it may take money, and it may take hard physical work. You need to be prepared for that—and keep on running to Jesus for strength.

Be prepared for awkwardness. There will be conversations in which there's a lot of silence, or you have nothing useful to say; when you don't know what to ask or how to comfort. Be prepared to feel that you are floundering as their friend.

Be prepared to weep. Are you prepared to enter into the full sadness of this loss? Not to stand off to the side as someone who is going to keep the control of distance. Are you prepared to come and sit in the ashes?

Be prepared to listen. Most grieving people *do* actually want to talk about their pain. Pain looks for outlets. But since it is deeply personal pain, it is shared with those who are trusted. Will you be a trustworthy person in the way you listen? If in doubt, say less. This is not a time for clever prescriptions for how to get out of the valley as quickly as possible—those who boast a rapid exit may find a brutal return later. We felt far more loved and understood by people who simply said things like, "I'm so sorry to hear that" than from people who tried to offer false comfort or reassurance.

Be prepared to remember. Would you put important dates and anniversaries in your calendar, setting yourself a reminder so that you can message and offer comfort around these times? For instance, our strongest memories are around the anniversaries of Jed's 12-week scan (when his diagnosis was detected), his birth, and his death. For families who have suffered miscarriages or stillbirths, their baby's due date may also be very poignant. But more broadly than this, would you commit to remembering that this grief will keep reverberating through your loved one's life for their whole lifetime? We've noticed that, in churches, when someone suffers something terrible, people tend to rally around them well in the early days; a sudden change and crisis motivates people. But as a new status quo emerges, the suffering one subtly drifts from the centre of people's awareness. This is understandable, as people are naturally concerned with the day to day. But if you are committing to walking together, please be prepared to keep remembering and not forgetting.

Be prepared to pray and to keep praying. Part of remembering is remembering these grieving ones before the Lord. Ask him to give healing where it can be given. Ask him to keep giving them strength, comfort, hope. Ask him to give you wisdom to love and support them as best you can. Ask him to work out his marvellous plans through this suffering, and to give those in the midst of it the eyes of faith to trust in God with all their hearts.

Be prepared to pursue and serve. Will you go beyond a polite text message saying "Please let me know if I can do anything", and take the initiative? Much of loving one another consists in the readiness to pursue people. We're not talking about overstepping boundaries, or of becoming a pest. We're talking about persevering initiative-taking. For grieving people, simple binary choices of help are better than open-ended ones. If you say, "Is there anything I can do to help?", it's so open-ended that they have to do the hard thinking, select from various options that might come to mind, and then perhaps write it all out back to you in a message. It feels too overwhelming. But if you say, "I'm going to the shops this morning; shall I pick you up some milk, biscuits, and a pizza?", it's an easy "yes or no" choice. It's also easier for you, since you are integrating care for your friends into your own daily routine. Some common areas of stress where you might consider offering a clear and simple choice of help are: shopping, cleaning, gardening, and any other practical things around the house you can think of. If they have other children, offer babysitting and playdates. We had hospital scans every fortnight during our pregnancy, and our church family really blessed us by arranging people to look after our girls each time, meaning that we could attend the scans together.

Be prepared to give. Do you enjoy cooking? Could you drop them round a hot meal? Could you drop them round a meal every Tuesday evening? Could you drop them a big batch of meals for the freezer? Do you *not* enjoy cooking? Could you buy them a nice ready meal from the supermarket instead? We have a precious memory of a delicious lunch we were able to buy ourselves one day while Jed was in hospital from the nearby Marks and Spencer food hall, with a generous gift card we'd been given. In the midst of a sad time, that meal still stands out as a real blessing. While we were pregnant, a kind couple took our children for an afternoon and sent us out for a wonderful afternoon tea. It was a taste of heaven's beauty, rest and feasting in an otherwise bitter and gruelling season. If you are in a position to, could you meet an expense that might have arisen as a result of the child's death? Jed's headstone, which testified to our hope in Jesus being the resurrection and the life, was paid for by a generous family member, who also paid for a family buffet after his thanksgiving service.

Be prepared to ask for help yourself. There is a dark side of caring sincerely; it is the danger of exhausting yourself to such a degree that you find yourself in a black hole. Watch that you don't try to be a saviour. We already have a Saviour, and his power and grace will be enough to see us through as we lean upon *him*—not you. Persisting in prayer for your grieving friends will keep you grounded in this truth. If you are a church leader, please look in particular at how you might enable a group, rather than an individual, to walk closely with those grieving.

We want to close with one more word from the New Testament:

> *But we do not want you to be uninformed, brothers,*
> *about those who are asleep, that you may not grieve as*
> *others do who have no hope. For since we believe that*
> *Jesus died and rose again, even so, through Jesus, God*
> *will bring with him those who have fallen asleep. For this*
> *we declare to you by a word from the Lord, that we who*
> *are alive, who are left until the coming of the Lord, will*
> *not precede those who have fallen asleep. For the Lord*
> *himself will descend from heaven with a cry of command,*
> *with the voice of an archangel, and with the sound of the*
> *trumpet of God. And the dead in Christ will rise first.*
> *Then we who are alive, who are left, will be caught up*

*together with them in the clouds to meet the Lord in the air, and so we will always be with the Lord. **Therefore encourage one another with these words.***

(1 Thessalonians 4 v 13-18)

That final statement is one clear place in the Bible where we are clearly told *what to say* to encourage one another in the face of grief. What is that encouragement? That Jesus lives, and he is coming back. This is wonderful news—news we need to keep calling to mind and reminding one another about. We will return to this in the final chapter. For now, let's make it our final point:

Be prepared to encourage one another with the truth that Jesus lives, and he will return to make all things right.

9. Why Won't Jesus Heal My Child?

From the moment we learned about Jed's problems, *we prayed earnestly.*

We prayed alone, together, and often with others in our church family. Many friends and family around the world joined us in praying. We fasted. We asked again and again that Jed would be healed; that we might attend our next scan to find a miraculous resolution of his developmental problems.

A few years prior, Christian friends of ours had received exactly the same diagnosis of megacystis in their son at the 12-week scan. They were advised to consider genetic testing and termination. They were counselled that if he survived to term he would die shortly after birth. They were told that studies showed that in those who were "genetically normal", spontaneous resolution of megacystis was only seen to occur in those with a bladder length of less than 15mm. Their son's bladder was already beyond this 15mm size at 12 weeks (as was Jed's). At 18 weeks, they held a prayer meeting for their son, and a scan two days later showed *a complete resolution of the problem.* Our friends asked the medical team if they were able to explain it, and they were not. All subsequent scans were normal, and they were discharged from foetal medicine before their son was born. God had *miraculously* answered their prayers and healed their child.

For us, however, the weeks went by, and Jed wasn't healed; the scans looked worse and worse.

As Jed's birth approached, we increasingly prayed that he might confound all expectations and live. We prayed that his little body would prove stronger than his scans indicated it might be. We prayed he might be able to breathe without assistance. The day of his birth arrived, and within minutes he had a breathing tube, was attached to a ventilator and had been transferred to neonatal intensive care.

Then, we prayed constantly that his breathing and other issues would improve so that he might eventually be able to come home with us, even if that included lots of medical support. But in fact, Jed relied on the breathing tube until the day he died.

Part of the journey of grief—certainly for those of us with faith in God—is the gnawing pain of *unanswered prayer*.

Perhaps you are reading this and right now you feel this weight, this inner troubledness. *If God is a mighty healer and a compassionate Father, why is my prayer for my child's healing going unanswered?* Perhaps you are reading this after your child has died. You still have a nagging doubt or even outrage at God for not only allowing their death but seemingly ignoring your heartfelt cries along the way. However thrilled you are for other people's health and happiness, it's hard to ignore this question: why did he heal or bless *them*, but not us? After all, if God is all-powerful, why couldn't he help our lovely little one? And if he's all-loving, why didn't he help us?

In this chapter we explore the painful angles of unanswered prayer. We start by asking, have we totally misunderstood

Jesus' character? And then we'll ask, is there a reason that Jesus withheld healing from us? Both these questions can utterly wreck our world if we don't honestly ask and strive to answer them.

DOESN'T JESUS CARE?

When we read the Bible, we can't miss the fact that Jesus heals. He has compassion—including compassion on those who ask for healing on behalf of their children. Think of the father who treks to see Jesus in John 4 v 46-54, whose son is healed. Think of the healing of Jairus' daughter (Matthew 9 v 18-26). This is the same Jesus who invites his people to come to him with all their burdens (Matthew 11 v 28). The Jesus who promises the unfailing attention of the Father towards those who trust him (John 14 v 6-7, 21, 23). So, we are quite right to pray boldly for healing.

However, Jesus never promises that he will heal everyone who asks for it in the timing they long for. Nor does Jesus, in the Bible, heal everyone. We tend to focus on the miracles because they are so remarkable, so staggeringly wonderful. We often forget that, for each child healed in the Bible, there would have been many lying sick in that region who were *not* healed by Jesus. In the famous account of Jesus healing the paralysed man in John 5, we're told that a *great number* of invalid and paralysed people used to lie in that very spot (John 5 v 3). Yet we aren't told of the others being healed. So we *aren't* given an entitlement to all healing in this life.

It's possible we have misunderstood Jesus without realising it. If we think Jesus might not have the power to heal, we are badly mistaken. If we think his heart is distant and uncaring, we are badly mistaken. And if we think that Jesus has promised healing to everyone in this life, we are again mistaken. What we need to see is that Jesus is indeed the King of love, who cares more than we can comprehend about those who suffer, and who has graciously given many healings to many people at different times—and that these are *signposts* and *previews* of the age to come. Then we are closer to seeing the true Jesus.

If you have sat in a cinema and seen a trailer for an upcoming movie, you will have had an impression within a few seconds of the themes, the plot, the characters. And then it's gone. If it was a good trailer, you think, "*I can't wait* for that movie to come out". That's what's going on with Jesus' miracles: it's as if Jesus is pulling back the screen separating earth from the kingdom of heaven, and giving us a glimpse of how glorious the future will be.

Jesus is the one who will bring heaven to earth. But he has not done it yet—not fully. Even the most remarkable miracles are only previews of the real substance yet to come. Even if Jed had been healed like our friends' son had, that healing would not have been final, as Jed would still have died at some point in the future. The whole world still needs fixing.

Jesus' miracles demonstrate that he has power to heal and that he deeply cares. They are not a guarantee that we will meet with miraculous healing in this life. But they *are* a guarantee of something even better that is still to come. We really came to rest in this, and we pray you might too. We prayed for healing, longing for the gift of a long life with Jed. But we rested in the fact that Jesus *does* care, and in the certain hope that beyond this broken age lies a resurrection life to come, in which sickness and the need for healing will be a thing of the past.

IS THIS A PUNISHMENT?

Deep in our hearts lurks a voice which says things like, "I've disappointed Jesus—that's why he hasn't answered my prayers." "I haven't led a good life recently, so God is punishing me." "I'm a bad Christian. Of course God isn't going to bless me."

What do all these inner dialogues have in common? A view of God where he doesn't give us what we want because we haven't given him what he wants. Or, to turn it around, a view where we give God a kind of invoice for our good services and expect something in return.

Strictly speaking, this is the voice of *unbelief*. We tend to think of "belief" as being about whether you believe God exists or not. But in the Bible, the question of belief or unbelief is not about the existence of God, but about *what God is actually, truly like*. The big problem with the religious leaders and Pharisees in Jesus' day was their *unbelief*: they all believed in God, but they had him all wrong. Jesus didn't fit their system of what God was like, and so they crucified him. Our first question above—"Doesn't Jesus care?"—was also at root about unbelief.

Many of us don't realise just how ferocious and subtle our battle with unbelief is. As an example, Anna was plagued with the thought that Jed's illness was a punishment because she had not been thrilled at our early pregnancy scan to learn that she was carrying twins (and God must have been disappointed with that). Dan was troubled by the thought that this was a punishment for not being an attentive, prayerful enough dad in the early pregnancy (and God must be disappointed). Unbelief assumes: God is like us, easily disappointed and endlessly fault-finding. Unbelief concludes: God hasn't given us what we want because we didn't give him what he wants. But this is not true!

There's a place in the Old Testament where God says:

Let the wicked forsake his way,
 and the unrighteous man his thoughts;
let him return to the LORD, that he may have compassion
 on him,
 and to our God, for he will abundantly pardon.
For my thoughts are not your thoughts,
 neither are your ways my ways, declares the LORD.
                              (Isaiah 55 v 7-8)

Do you see? God's readiness to move towards sinners in love is what makes his ways and thoughts profoundly *unlike* ours. You and I *have* done things that would disappoint God, even things that would provoke God's anger—*if he were like us*. But he is not. He has compassion on all who turn to him. Jesus said that he came to call *sinners*, not people who have it all sorted (Mark 2 v 17).

Without looking to Jesus and depending on him, our sin does indeed keep us from relationship with God. But Jesus came to call and forgive sinners by dying for us on the cross. If we are trusting in him, then all God's anger at our sin has been satisfied, used up. In Christ nothing will ever keep us from the Father.

We have to confront our unbelief. Any thought which is saying that God is ignoring us, or disappointed with us, because of our sin, has an utterly false idea of God. God came for sinners! If you are trusting in Jesus, when suffering comes our way you can boldly say, "For which of my sins did Jesus not die?" When that terrible thought comes knocking at your door, "Your child died because of your sin", you can chase it away with the truth: "No, there is no sin of mine which Jesus did not pay for on his cross. And I know this because Jesus is alive. Nothing can separate me from the love of God, ever."

There is therefore now no condemnation for those who are in Christ Jesus. (Romans 8 v 1)

DID I NOT HAVE ENOUGH FAITH?

With this in mind, we're able to respond to another truly crushing thought: "They weren't healed because I didn't have enough faith."

Do you see that this is the same pattern as what we have been considering? "God must be disappointed. I must have failed his test." These are words of unbelief—since the truth is that if I am in Christ then God is delighted with me. I am his child. I am a treasure and a pleasure to him.

There are many places where Jesus addresses people with the words, "O you of little faith", especially in Matthew's Gospel (6 v 30; 8 v 26; 14 v 31; 16 v 8). Here's a question for us: why do we so often assume that he says this with a scowl of annoyance? What if it is a term of nurturing affection?

A father might call his son "little man" as a term of endearment. The boy might get distracted by a dog in the park and fall off his bike. As he picks him up, his dad says, "Why did you worry about the dog, little man?" He's not scolding; he's nurturing. In the same way, each time Jesus says, "O you of little faith", it is in a context where he is teaching, helping, or about to save. They are words of encouragement!

Jesus also said that faith as small as a mustard seed could move mountains (Matthew 17 v 20). Why? Because faith is not some inner quality we have, but our confidence *in* God. What really matters is not the size or strength of your faith—it is *who* you have faith *in*. And God delights in his people as they turn to him in faith, however small and feeble that faith is.

You may be thinking, "Ok—God isn't angry at me. But my small faith has *not* moved mountains. So what's going on?" What about all those verses which seem to promise anything we want if we have enough faith?

> *And whatever you ask in prayer, you will receive, if you have faith. (Matthew 21 v 22)*

The point of promises like this one is to invite us to pray boldly, since nothing is impossible for God, and he is our loving Father. When we put our trust in him, however faintly, we are acknowledging that he can do anything. And so, *in principle, whatever* we ask—however outrageous it may appear—we will receive.

Yet we don't always receive everything we ask for. Why? *Because sometimes our Father gives us something better.*

THE FATHER'S LOVE

The apostle Paul wrote in 2 Corinthians 12 of a "thorn" in his flesh—an unspecified suffering that was a great torment to him. "Three times I pleaded with the Lord about this, that it should leave me", he tells us in verse 8. So why did God not answer Paul's prayer? Because he was allowing this suffering for Paul's good.

> *But he said to me, "My grace is sufficient for you, for my power is made perfect in weakness." Therefore I will boast all the more gladly of my weaknesses, so that the power of Christ may rest upon me. For the sake of Christ, then, I am content with weaknesses, insults, hardships, persecutions, and calamities. For when I am weak, then I am strong. (2 Corinthians 12 v 9-10)*

Suffering is part of the way our Father shapes and refines us. In Paul's case, he prevented him from becoming conceited (v 7) and gave him a greater sense of God's love and power within him. We, too, will find that there are all kinds of nooks and crannies of self-righteousness, pride, and other sins, which God gently smokes out of us—not in a "crime and punishment" way but with the care and love of a master craftsman. And, like Paul, we will find that the more emptied we are of ourselves, the more we can be filled by him.

God has plans for us that are *better* than the plans we could make for ourselves. He has different plans for each of us, doing different things in all our lives. Our Father clearly had things he wanted to do in our lives through Jed's life and death that were not part of his plan for the friends we mentioned at the start of the chapter. Jed's death hurt deeply, yet we can say with Paul that we now boast all the more in Christ.

One of C.S. Lewis's most famous quotations about suffering is as follows:

> *One can imagine a sentient picture, after being rubbed and scraped and re-commenced for the tenth time, wishing that it were only a thumb-nail sketch whose making was over in a minute. In the same way, it is natural for us to wish that God had designed for us a less glorious and less arduous destiny; but then we are wishing not for more love but for less. (The Problem of Pain, p 34)*

As Christians, our pain is actually *proof* of the Father's loyal love. Everything in our lives is for our good, from our Father's hand. This is a tremendous comfort when the pain is unbearable.

Nevertheless, it can be hard to get your head around. To truly see God's goodness in suffering, we need to ask one more question.

WHY WAS JESUS' PRAYER NOT ANSWERED?

Jesus is in the Garden of Gethsemane. He knows he is about to be arrested. He knows he will shortly be condemned, mocked, abused and crucified. And so he prays:

Father, all things are possible for you. Remove this cup from me. Yet not what I will, but what you will.

(Mark 14 v 36)

Jesus is fully human; he experiences the dread and sorrow of this hour. The "cup" he talks of is a biblical metaphor for a time of terrible punishment and suffering: Jesus is speaking about the cross. He asks for this "cup" to be "removed". And do you see this: *what he asks for, he does not receive.* Remember that there is no question of the Father's love for Jesus, and no doubt over Jesus' perfect faith in and obedience to the Father. And yet, Jesus' prayer in his darkest hour goes unanswered. Why?

So that our prayers might never go unanswered. Because Jesus *did* suffer and die and rise—because the cup was *not* taken from him—we can be taken most surely to intimacy with the Father. Jesus himself is the way to God. Aren't we glad that Jesus' prayer was *not* answered? Otherwise, death would still be undefeated. Sins would remain unforgiven. There would be no hope of a future age of all things put right. God gave something better.

On the morning of 8th July 2019, we prayed fervently that God might yet do some miracle and help Jed to live. At lunchtime that day his breathing tube was going to be removed. Despite the excellent medical care he had received, it had become clear that Jed's body could not sustain him. As we prayed, we remembered Jesus at prayer. His unanswered prayer comforts us when our longings are poured out to God. Firstly, Jesus knows human experience to the very extreme. He knows what the darkest hour is like. Secondly, we know from his own work of suffering that God will indeed unfold everything according to his good plan. We can't see it at the time, but we can trust God to bring incredible beauty and redemption out of suffering. He did it with Jesus' sufferings and he will do it with ours.

Jesus' unanswered prayer guarantees a wonderful "one-way valve" to God's dealings with us. Through Jesus' suffering and death we have become children of God. God's answers to our prayers can only flow one way to us: only good will be done to us, ultimately, all the days of our lives.

> *And we know that for those who love God all things work together for good. (Romans 8 v 28)*

We can't see it yet, but we can wait confident of this. Jesus cares. He is powerful. He is not angry at us, and he has promised to put all things right.

FOLLOWING JESUS IN UNANSWERED PRAYER

In one sense, Jesus' prayer *was* answered. He said, "Your will be done". Jesus' desire was most deeply the desire of his Father. Jesus was not being cruelly overruled here; he wanted his Father's good will to unfold. In the same way, to learn the way of Jesus is to learn this way of praying as a true child. To lay our desires before God, accompanied with a heartfelt request that his good will be done—since we are convinced, from the work of Jesus, that the Father's will is really *good*. If it is indeed true that my Father loves me more truly and wisely than I (or anyone else) love myself, then I want my Father's will to be done.

To put it another way, if we trust that our Father really is good, then when we pray "Your will be done", we are acknowledging that *if we were all-wise, all-powerful, and all-loving*, as our Father is, then his will (be it a full healing, or no change, or something else) *is the exact situation that we would ask for.*

And this is how we arrive at the way of living alongside an inconsolable longing. To know that our Father is good holds us within the warm sunshine of hope.

If Jesus is true, and if he is who the Bible portrays him to be, then he is fully in control, and he will somehow restore the fortunes of his broken-hearted people to an extent which will bring us to *shout* with laughter and joy (Psalm 126 v 5). The hard thing is that when our prayers go unanswered, we live in the gap between the painful loss and the full understanding of *why* the Lord allowed this; what his ultimate good plan is.

It's for this reason that the Bible emphasises the theme of waiting and hoping in the Lord. "Those who hope in me will not be disappointed", says God (Isaiah 49 v 23 NIV). After the prophet Isaiah foretold the suffering and death of Jesus hundreds of years beforehand (Isaiah 52 v 13 – 53 v 12), his very next words were these incredible ones: "Sing, O barren one!" (Isaiah 54 v 1). The point is this: the most shamed, disappointed members of the community at those times—women unable to have children—were to be the *first* to rejoice after the death and resurrection of Jesus. In Jesus, God has delivered on all of his wonderful promises. The painful waiting and longing will end and give way to joyous shouts. The greater the pain, the greater the joy.

So we go by faith, not by sight. Our Lord doesn't promise universal healing here and now, but he does promise sufficient grace for every step of the journey home. And he promises resurrection. In Jesus, there really is a way to live with inconsolable longing in the warm and steady sunshine of hope. As we follow Jesus, we learn to pray boldly, "Please heal, Lord!" We learn to say most sincerely, "But your will be done, loving Father." And we learn to wait with utter assurance that our Father will only do us good, for ever.

10. What Happens to Little Ones When they Die?

Our son Jed is buried in the children's area of Saltwell Cemetery in Gateshead, UK. His grave is surrounded by the small graves of other babies and children. As you would expect, these gravesides are among the best cared for in the whole cemetery. Many are as filled with decorations as the space allows. Sometimes, parents will kindly bring flowers and decorate *every single grave* in the children's area. There is a tangible yearning on that small field to express the love that parents were not able to shower on their child, since his or her life ended too soon.

What's most tragic amid this yearning is the lack of certainty about where that child is now. If people believe that their child was a mere bundle of molecules, organised for a while as a human being, but now decomposing into something else, they certainly don't show it. Without question, people would rather choose to believe that their dead babies are now angels, sending them feathers on the wind as reminders of their lives. But they're *not sure*.

This chapter is about an awful question to put into words:

Dan & Anna Martin

what happens to babies when they die? It's a question many of us find it hard to look directly at: where is my little one now? Will I ever see him or her again? Let's remember that, for most of history, most people had personal experience of losing at least one child. When we walk through the older sections of the cemeteries in Gateshead, which date back well over a hundred years, we notice very many young children's gravestones. There is a strange comfort from knowing that *our suffering isn't unique*, and that many, many other parents before us have had to think about this question.

There is no chapter of the Bible that tackles this specific question head-on, and consequently we readily acknowledge that some biblically faithful Christians will draw different conclusions to those we share below. The death of our son Jed caused us to think about this question ever so sincerely—to dig deep into Scripture, grappling with any and all passages that at least make oblique references to this subject. The conclusion we came to—that Jesus keeps little ones safe with him when they die—is something we have repeatedly taken apart, put back together again, and rested in. But our ultimate rest is not in our own reasoning or our own answers; it's in our knowledge that God is *always good*, and that he will do what is right.

We hope that through reading this chapter you will, with us, be comforted by him.

SALVATION IN JESUS

What *is* the Bible clear on? We need to make two observations before we dig in properly. Firstly, we saw in chapter 7 that human life begins at conception: you are *fully* a person, a unique being in the universe, from then onwards. This is our stable starting point for the rest of this chapter. Secondly, this means that everything the Bible has to say about people, and what happens to them after death, applies to babies who die— including unborn babies, since they too are people.

With those things in mind, here is a crucial point: all humans are held to account for what they have done with their knowledge of God. Biblical Christianity has always believed the following;

1. *All humans naturally turn away from God and therefore cannot save themselves (Romans 3 v 23).*
2. *Jesus is our only hope for salvation (Acts 4 v 12; John 14 v 6).*
3. *Jesus saves **all** those who have faith in him (John 3 v 16).*

What about a baby, too young for faith in Jesus to have ever been formed? No one wants to say that a baby goes to hell. But neither would a sincere Christian want to say that there is any way of being saved apart from Jesus Christ. It's easy to see why some Christians simply avoid thinking hard about the question of what happens to babies when they die.

But let's press on in the confident knowledge that God is good. We need to ask: what does it mean that humans are held to account for what they have done with their knowledge of God? The Bible is clear that God has revealed himself in two ways to people everywhere. Firstly, in the *created world* around us:

For what can be known about God is plain to them, because God has shown it to them. For his invisible attributes, namely, his eternal power and divine nature, have been clearly perceived, ever since the creation of the

world, in the things that have been made. So they are
without excuse. (Romans 1 v 19-20)

Secondly, in our *consciences*:

The work of the law is written on their hearts, while
their conscience also bears witness, and their conflicting
thoughts accuse or even excuse them. (Romans 2 v 15)

Our conscience is like God's watermark within us—a mark of his existence and ownership. If you do something wrong, even if no one else sees, your conscience is the inner voice which *accuses* you: "You shouldn't have done that". Yet because of sin, our consciences become twisted into tools which we often use to *excuse* our wrongdoing: "I was right to swear at that driver, since they pulled out in front of me". Our sense of right and wrong becomes oriented around ourselves. We live in God's world without reference to him; as Romans 1 v 18 puts it, we "suppress the truth".

When we realise this, we see why Jesus' gospel is such good and urgent news for everyone to hear and be invited to believe: in Jesus there is forgiveness and new life for all who turn to him.

The question for us is, how does this apply to young children and unborn babies?

WITHOUT EXCUSE?

The Bible talks about an age when a young child knows "how to refuse the evil and choose the good" (Isaiah 7 v 15-16)—in other words, an age at which a child is capable of making moral choices. It doesn't specify what this age is. But it implies that there is an age before which a young child does *not* have the moral capacity to perceive and suppress the truth about God. And that God knows this.

Following this logic, we came to the conclusion that when little ones die without this capacity for moral knowledge of God yet formed, there is nothing separating them from the loving-kindness of God; there is no condemnation. John Piper, a respected pastor and writer, agrees:

The "therefore" at the end [of Romans 1 v 20] says that mankind would seem to have an excuse if they had not seen clearly in nature what God is like. And so, because I don't think little babies can process nature and make conclusions about God's grace, glory or justice, it seems they would fall into the category of still having an excuse ... God will not condemn them because he wants to manifest openly and publicly that he does not condemn those who did not have the mental capacities to put their faith in him. (John Piper, "Why do you believe that infants who die go to heaven?", desiringgod.org)

We find a comforting example of this in Deuteronomy. The people of Israel are told that they will not enter the promised land, on account of their faithlessness. However, God adds:

*As for your little ones ... and your children, who today have **no knowledge of good or evil**, they shall go in there. And to them I will give it, and they shall possess it.*
(Deuteronomy 1 v 39)

This verse affirms what we are saying: there is an age of moral responsibility, which God knows. And his *favour*—not his condemnation—rests upon those who are not yet able to know and trust him.

Let's pause for a moment to summarise what we have said thus far. We recognise that we are probing the limits of what the Bible speaks clearly and directly about. These two statements are clear from Scripture:

1. *Little babies who die are people.*
2. *People who suppress the knowledge of God are condemned.*

And this is a conclusion we believe we can logically draw:

3. *Since little babies died before they formed the capacity to suppress the knowledge of God, they are not condemned.*

Now we need to add a fourth point:

4. *But little babies who die still need saving.*

THE GIFT OF SALVATION

What do we mean? We have just said that little babies who die do not die sinning against God. Yet they *do* need saving from the whole broken age into which they were born, from the sinful nature of the human race. They need saving from out of death! How can this happen, if they were not old enough to put their faith in Jesus? Let us find comfort in this truth:

5. *Salvation is always a gift from God.*

People need personal faith in Jesus to be saved. But where does that faith come from? Ephesians 2 v 8 tells us that it is a "gift of God". The same chapter writes that Christians are those who were spiritually "dead" but whom God has made spiritually "alive" (v 5). The point: spiritually dead people have no means of saving themselves. But God is the giver of life. He gives new eyes, new hearts, new life to his people— enabling them to see how great his love is, *enabling them to trust him personally*. Saving faith doesn't come from us—it always comes from God as a gift. And if saving faith is always a gift from God, then it is a gift that God can give to babies and unborn children.

Does this mean that these most broken and overlooked ones were known and precious to God before time ever began?

Does this mean that Christ at the cross redeemed unborn children who would die—along with all his other people—by his blood? That by his blood they too have received the full inheritance of new life in the presence of God?

Does this mean that God will bring these little ones to a realisation of what colossal privileges they have, and to a personal faith in Jesus worked by the Spirit? That they will come to know the love of the Father, and enjoy him eternally?

While there is no chapter in the Bible which deals directly and at length with these questions, we believe that we can be confident to answer yes, yes, yes. Now we glimpse again what we saw in chapter 5: that little ones who pass so briefly through this age are actually richly blessed. Our God saves. If he has done everything to save *us* when we were spiritually dead, then why would we doubt that he can do everything to save babies who die?

To repeat, the Bible does not speak about this directly. But in light of what it does teach, we believe that the work of Jesus to achieve eternal life for his people included achieving life for tiny little people who died too young for faith yet to have formed. What the Father has planned, and the Lord Jesus has achieved, and the Holy Spirit applies, is this: *life*. God—the Father, the Son, and the Holy Spirit—saves little ones who die and gives them *life*.

Here is what we are saying so far. We will return to this statement again:

Little children who die—born or unborn—go straight into the presence of Jesus.

DAVID'S LOST SONS

If you are still in doubt, consider the story of David (as John MacArthur's book *Safe in the Father's Arms* encouraged us to do). The Bible records that David lost three of his sons, all tragically. One of his grown sons, Absalom, killed another, Amnon (2 Samuel 13). Later, Absalom himself was killed, and David was devastated (2 Samuel 18). But David also had a baby son who became sick and then died (2 Samuel 12). In this case, David showed his grief by praying and fasting earnestly while the baby was sick; but when he learned of the child's death, he started to eat again.

When his adult son died, David *started* grieving. When his infant son died, David *stopped* grieving. Why? David's answer is bound up in what he thinks about the future.

> *While the child was still alive, I fasted and wept, for I said, "Who knows whether the LORD will be gracious to me, that the child may live?" But now he is dead. Why should I fast? Can I bring him back again? I shall go to him, but he will not return to me. (2 Samuel 12 v 22-23)*

Absalom died a grown man, shaking his fist at God and doing his utmost to seize glory for himself. David loved Absalom dearly and was devastated at this loss. Yet when his baby died, David said, "I will go to him". In other words, David was asserting that he would see the child again. His loss was not final.

It's not clear how fully the glorious hope of resurrection life had been revealed to David, who lived about a thousand years before Jesus. The Old Testament frequently speaks of a "place of the dead" (or Sheol, e.g. Genesis 37 v 35), but it also glimpses the resurrection age (e.g. Daniel 12 v 2). So, whether David means "I will go to the place of the dead and see my child again", or "I will see my child in eternal life beyond death in the presence of God", can't be concluded definitively from this immediate context.

Elsewhere, though, David writes with a real clarity about the future certainty of life beyond death. For instance, in Psalm 16 v 10-11 David explicitly says that his future does *not* lie in Sheol, the place of the dead, but in the joyous presence of God. This means that we needn't conclude that David simply has in mind some shadowy "place of the dead" when he thinks of his dead infant son. After all, if that was the case, he could have said something similar about Absalom.

Instead, David rests in the fact that he will see his baby again, when he "goes to him", to dwell with God eternally after his own death. David does not and cannot say this about Absalom, since Absalom had rejected this eternal future for himself.

David's words are consistent with this chapter's main point: *little children who die—born or unborn—go straight into the presence of Jesus.* We can be confident that it is the presence of *Jesus* since Jesus returned to rule on God's throne after his resurrection—that is where he is now. To be in the presence of God is to be in the presence of the risen Lord Jesus.

If you are troubled that we have, in our reflections, swum too far from the shoreline of what Scripture clearly teaches, here is how we find our footing again. When our questions go beyond what God has made clearly known, we can trust that God, the judge of all the earth, will "do what is right" (Genesis 18 v 25). Our hope does not lie in how well we understand our Bible. Our hope does not lie in us knowing what "right" is. Our hope lies in the fact that the living God always knows and always does what is right.

OUR LORD'S BEST JEWELS

Infant loss was a common part of normal life until very recent times. Precisely because losing a child was so common, it wasn't written about directly very much. But there are fragments— and these prove to be of great comfort for those of us who feel in need of steady footing as we consider where our child is now.

One such fragment is found in an ancient document called the *Apology of Aristides*, a defence of Christianity presented to the Roman emperor some time in the second century AD. In the midst of describing what Christians are like, Aristides says this:

> *And when a child has been born to one of them, they give thanks to God; and if moreover it happen to die in childhood, they give thanks to God the more, as for one who has passed through the world without sins.*
> *(Apology of Aristides, Syriac version, section 15)*

Remember, Aristides' goal here was not to put together a book or speech about infant loss; he only mentions it in passing. But the very fact that the loss of children gets a mention shows us the following:

> 1. *It was a sufficiently common experience to form part of the general description of a Christian in the Roman Empire at this time.*

2. *Christians were sufficiently united in their views about what happened to children who died for this statement to sit alongside other uncontroversial statements about Christians' views and practices.*
3. *This was the case from extremely early on in the Christian church.*

A more emotive example are the letters of the 17th-century Scottish pastor Samuel Rutherford.

Rutherford personally knew both the deep pain of infant loss and the rich comfort that the Lord Jesus gives: his first wife had died young, as had their two infant daughters. Of the seven children he had with his second wife, six would die during his lifetime. He wrote the following to Lady Gaitgirth, a mother who had lost several of her children at a young age:

Cast the burden of your sweet babes upon Christ, and lighten your heart, by laying your all upon Him. He will be their God ...

They are not lost to you, they are laid up so well as that they are coffered in heaven where our Lord's best jewels lie. They are all free goods that are there, death can have no law to arrest any thing that is within the walls of the new Jerusalem.

Similarly, he wrote to Lady Kenmure after the death of her infant daughter:

Ye have lost a child: nay she is not lost to you who is found to Christ. She is not sent away, but only sent before, like unto a star, which going out of our sight doth not die and vanish, but shineth in another hemisphere. We see her not, yet she doth shine in another country.

It is a great comfort indeed to know that our earnest reflections on the Bible today about what happens to young children when they die are consistent with the convictions of Christians of previous generations, those who were well familiar with the loss of little ones. *Little children who die—born or unborn—go straight into the presence of Jesus.*

WE WILL GO TO THEM

This really changes everything. Our little ones are already safe with God. If we receive life and forgiveness through faith in Jesus *ourselves*, then we will go to them, like David, and be with them for all eternity. Jesus' triumph means that we will one day hold them, know them, love them and be loved by them, and never be parted again. We will see their bodies and ours restored to wholeness and perfection. We can do nothing more to add to their safety and joy, since they are in the Lord's presence. They are known and can never be forgotten for all eternity, even if a day will come when no one knows of them here on earth.

The morning after Jed died, we sent this message to family and friends:

Dear all,

There has been so much grace, comfort and peace this weekend. God walked with us through the valley of the shadow of death and we praise him for this. We have some very precious memories. Thank you for your prayers and messages.

Jed was honoured by visits from all the aunts, uncles, cousins and grandparents who were in a position to travel.

On Saturday, Dan and I were together when we saw his eyes open for the first time which was very moving. And for the rest of his time with us, Jed blessed us by opening his eyes when he was in Dan and I's arms.

Yesterday Jed was extubated at about 3pm and for the next three hours had his eyes open as he had cuddles from us both and Lois, Esther and Ethan. There were tears, prayers and singing. He died very peacefully just over three hours later with just Dan and I present.

We washed him, dressed and swaddled him and left him looking beautiful... Not that he cares, given where he now is. He died looking into our faces, and awoke to Jesus'. Praise Him! We are so grateful for this certain hope which takes some of the sting out of the awfulness of death.

We miss him.

With lots of love and gratitude for you for standing with us,

Dan, Anna, Lois, Esther and Ethan xx

11. From Tears to Shouts of Joy

All chapters lead here

Thank you for coming to this chapter. Without this chapter, we don't think anything else in the book can quite make sense. Without the substance of what this chapter is about, our story and yours is nothing more than a tragedy. In fact, it's worse than a tragedy—it's just a meaningless set of events on planet Earth. Without the resurrection of Jesus, there is no ultimate point of coherence, no ultimate meaning, no ultimate justice, no ultimate resolution, no hope.

This isn't the place for an explanation of why we can be confident that the resurrection is true—for that, you might like to try *The Son Rises: Historical Evidence for the Resurrection of Jesus* by William Lane Craig, or *The Case for Easter* by Lee Strobel. Our purpose here is less intellectual and more personal. If Jesus is alive, what difference does it really make to us, and to our experience of loss?

A HOPE TO HOLD ONTO

Jesus' resurrection changes *absolutely everything*. But if we don't immediately see this, we are in good company. The news of Jesus' empty tomb was initially met with confusion, fear, and trembling. Here is Jesus' friend Thomas when the other disciples tell him they have seen Jesus alive:

> *Now Thomas, one of the Twelve, called the Twin, was not with them when Jesus came. So the other disciples told him, "We have seen the Lord." But he said to them, "Unless I see in his hands the mark of the nails, and place my finger into the mark of the nails, and place my hand into his side, I will never believe."*
>
> (John 20 v 24-25)

Was Thomas an emotionally detached intellectual sceptic? Not at all. He was like you and me. He was in the midst of life-breaking grief. He had just seen his dear friend and leader Jesus, to whom he had pledged his life (John 11 v 16), crucified and buried. He could not bear the thought of being given false hope, and so he refused to believe that Jesus was alive unless he saw for himself.

Perhaps you feel like Thomas. You're so full of grief that you're struggling to believe in the truths we've shared in this book, in case those hopes too are dashed. Maybe you *do* believe, but you feel like you're free-floating, all at sea. If only there were something you could touch and hold on to.

Here is what happens next in Thomas's story:

> *Eight days later, his disciples were inside again, and Thomas was with them. Although the doors were locked, Jesus came and stood among them and said, "Peace be with you." Then he said to Thomas, "Put your finger here, and see my hands; and put out your hand, and place it in my side. Do not disbelieve, but believe." Thomas answered him, "My Lord and my God!" Jesus said to him, "Have*

*you believed because you have seen me? Blessed are those
who have not seen and yet have believed."*

(John 20 v 26-29)

The risen Lord Jesus comes to Thomas and gives him something
to touch. Jesus knows with a particular tenderness the hearts of
those crushed with grief. He delights to make himself known to
weary ones, not as an abstract concept but as who he really is:
the personal, living, hope-bringing Lord. Hope does not rest in
our ability to hope. Jesus himself is the hope—and that hope is
more solid than anything else could be. As we're about to see.

AN IRREVERSIBLE SEQUENCE

In all our chapters thus far, we have shared many things which
bring hope; but only if Jesus really lives. Even the wonder of
Jesus raising Lazarus back to life (John 11), an account we've
considered in this book, cries out for a further resolution.
Lazarus soon received a death threat because of his association
with Jesus (John 12 v 10). In due time, Lazarus would die, as
would his family and friends. The world still needed fixing after
Lazarus was raised! But at last the glorious news is here: Jesus
died *and rose.*

His resurrection is not only about his own victory over
death. It is not only about his own immortal physical body
living on for ever. Here is why our hope is so solid when it is
founded on Jesus: because his resurrection *is the beginning of a
whole new age.* It is about Jesus' own victory being shared with
all his people and all the created world.

One place where the New Testament unpacks the
significance of Jesus' resurrection is 1 Corinthians 15. Read
it through and you'll see that Jesus' resurrection has begun an
irreversible sequence:

1. *Jesus rose from the dead (v 3-8).*
2. *He will return (v 23).*
3. *He will raise all his people (v 22-23).*
4. *He will be victorious and rule over all things (v 24-25)…*
5. *…including being victorious over death (v 26).*

In Jesus, God has begun his new creation. Jesus is spoken of as the "firstfruits" of what is coming (v 23). In Britain we talk of the "first daffodil of spring": when you see a daffodil in February, you recognise that spring is inevitably on its way, even if it may still feel like winter. Jesus' resurrection is like that: it is the irreversible pledge that God is delivering on all his promises to put things right.

Here is just one passage that describes what the results of that final victory will be:

> *Then I saw a new heaven and a new earth, for the first heaven and the first earth had passed away … And I heard a loud voice from the throne saying, "Behold, the dwelling place of God is with man. He will dwell with them, and they will be his people, and God himself will be with them as their God. He will wipe away every tear from their eyes, and death shall be no more, neither shall there be mourning, nor crying, nor pain any more, for the former things have passed away." And he who was seated on the throne said, "Behold, I am making all things new."*
> *(Revelation 21 v 1, 3-5)*

This long-promised and awaited world without sickness, death, tears, grief, conflict, disaster, sin or betrayal is now *a world which is most definitely coming*, through the death and resurrection of Jesus.

THE ANSWER TO OUR QUESTIONS

Life as we know it holds many unanswered questions, many uncertainties. Even the happiest moments in our lives can't be held. All we have is the present, and then the memories, and eventually they fade too as our lives end. Trying to hold onto life is like trying to hold onto a handful of sand. Countless artists, musicians and writers have grappled with expressing the painful weight of this. Why do we long for enduring meaning, when we're seemingly cursed with transience? If we are just a bunch of molecules, why do we grieve? If death is just normal, part of the grand plan of our genes to preserve and propagate themselves, why does it feel profoundly wrong?

The answer to all our uncertainty truly is: the risen Lord Jesus. In his death, the meaninglessness, brokenness, sin, evil, pain and transience of this whole age has been put to death. In his life, a whole new age has been irreversibly established.

Yet the risen Lord Jesus is not only the answer to previously unresolved questions. He himself is the glorious hope for the future. What is promised is so good that we may actually have a hard time daring to believe it. We struggle to imagine how something so good could ever be. It's like waking up as a child in a wonderful new place on holiday: as we reflect on Jesus' resurrection we will keep noticing new, different, wonderful things. We realise that we are living in a whole new landscape, one coloured to all horizons with the promise of new life in all its fullness.

- There will be a day when we will no longer grieve.
- There will be a day when our mourning will stop, when our tears will no longer flow.
- There will be a day when we will no longer have things to be sad about.

- There will be a day when we will laugh true, uncomplicated laughter.
- There will be a day when we will enjoy whole, profoundly intimate, fun, secure relationships with other people.
- There will be a day when we will live without weapons, CCTV, passwords, locks, lawyers, doctors, pharmacists, hospitals, social care or the police. We will be perfectly safe without those things.

Because Jesus lives, that day is now coming. We keep waking up to new and wonderful details of the coming age. When we notice daffodils, our attention is redirected towards spring, and our spirits are lifted from the cold and grey of winter. In the same way, when we fix our eyes on the living Jesus, our attention is redirected towards life in all its fullness, and our spirits begin to be lifted from the griefs and frustrations of life here and now.

FROM PENDING TO ACTIVE

Here is another way to think about life and history on this side of Jesus' resurrection. When you place an order on a website, you might get a notification saying, "Your order has been received and is now pending". Then there's that exciting moment when it moves from pending to active: "Your order has been dispatched and is out for delivery". Pending means it *will* happen. Active means *it's happening*. Because of Jesus' resurrection, all the promises of God have jumped from pending to active.

The Bible's storyline begins with a perfect creation in which the first humans lived in joyful relationship with God, one another, and creation (Genesis 1 – 2). For short, we can call this "Eden", after the garden that was there. In Genesis 3,

Adam and Eve doubt and disobey God; in other words, they sin. And sin causes the breaking of all these relationships. Now humans are separated from God by their sin and separated from one another by their sin; and in fact all of creation has become broken and frustrated. Eden is lost. The rest of the storyline shows God making one gracious promise after another (beginning, in fact, already in Genesis 3 v 15) that Eden will be somehow restored. One promise after another is made, and yet they seem to be left *pending*—like a delivery that hasn't yet left the warehouse.

Fast-forward through the Bible, and the New Testament is emphatic that, in Jesus, all of God's promises are fulfilled (e.g. Luke 24 v 26-27, 44-47; 2 Corinthians 1 v 20).

- We might say that in the *birth* of Jesus the promises moved from "pending" to "dispatched". There's a fitting celebration of angels and stars in the sky announcing the birth of the King at Christmas.
- In the *death and resurrection* of Jesus the promises are "delivered", in the most unexpected and ironic way. Jesus utters his final words from the cross, "It is finished" (John 19 v 30).
- Jesus' *crucified and risen* body is the package delivered, the triumphant reality. Through him, people are welcomed back into right relationship with God and with one another, and privileged with the hope of a perfect physical new creation—a new Eden.

As an example, think of Jesus' famous miracle of turning water into wine. Back in the book of Isaiah, God had promised to make a feast for all his people, one which would be particularly characterised by fine wine (Isaiah 25 v 6). This is no ordinary feast but a promise of the new creation, as the very next thought reveals:

> *He will swallow up death for ever;*
> *and the LORD GOD will wipe away tears from all faces.*
> *(Isaiah 25 v 8)*

In John 2, Jesus comes to a wedding and miraculously produces wine which is praised because it is so fine. It's no mere party trick. The point is that Jesus himself is the bringer of the long-awaited new age, where death and mourning are no more. What was pending is now active. We're told that through this miracle Jesus showed his glory and his disciples believed in him (John 2 v 11). And soon after Jesus showed this at that wedding, he *delivered* it in full through his death and resurrection. Death has indeed been "swallowed up".

Jesus has delivered on God's promises. And life for us *now* is living with those promises partly—but not yet fully— unboxed.

GRIEF REHARMONISED

Christians are people of the future. We know what is coming, and we know that through our Lord we will be a part of it. We taste the joy to come in part—but not yet fully. We still feel grief ever so painfully. But we don't grieve quite like those who don't know Jesus do.

> *But we do not want you to be uninformed, brothers,*
> *about those who are asleep [i.e., those who have died],*
> *that you may not grieve as others do who have no hope.*
> *For since we believe that Jesus died and rose again, even*
> *so, through Jesus, God will bring with him those who have*
> *fallen asleep. (1 Thessalonians 4 v 13-14)*

In Jesus, grief can't be quite the same again because it just does not have the final word. Death, and this whole broken age, has been overcome by Jesus.

The effect is something like playing a minor chord on an instrument. If you sit at a piano and play a C minor chord, it sounds sad. But music harmony has this interesting aspect whereby the lowest note being played, the bass note, has control over how a chord feels. Normally, a C minor chord will have a low C note as its bass, and so it will sound purely sad. But if you were to move the lowest note to, say, A flat, you will notice that although the chord sounds similar (you have after all, only changed one note), the new bass note profoundly changes the feel and effect. It's been reharmonised.

In the same way, Jesus' resurrection is the new bass note of our grief. We aren't living in some make-believe world where pain and grief don't affect us. Life is, in one sense, still the same. This book exists because we share the bitter pain of a sick or dead child. But Jesus' resurrection in the *past* guarantees the whole new Eden of the *future*, and thus the reharmonisation of the *present*.

This is why that same passage in 1 Thessalonians repeats its urging to "*encourage* one another with these words" (1 Thessalonians 4 v 18; 5 v 11). The correct use of the wonderful news of the resurrection is encouragement: it is meant to return us to hope. As we live waiting for the full unboxing of what is to come, we will need to encourage one another repeatedly with the reality of Jesus' resurrection. Keep sounding the new, joyous bass note. "I don't know how I can bear it, *but* Jesus lives and so I know that somehow my tears will end one day." "I see how hard this is for you, and I'm so sorry. *But* Jesus lives and so I will pray for you in confidence that you will start to see glimmers of hope in him."

We will often find this hard to do, awkward, unfamiliar. Other people will be more fluent at it than us. But realise this: *there is no greater encouragement than the resurrection of Jesus.*

No one should be asking you to dismiss your pain, to act like it's not as bad as it is, or to suppress it. Actually, we're *more* able to feel and bear the full weight of it because we are anchored in the knowledge that this age of weeping is passing away. We can accept the heaviness of it because we know we won't have to carry it for ever.

THE JOY TO COME

The *risen* Lord Jesus is the one who promises himself, personally, to "wipe away every tear" from his people's eyes (Revelation 21 v 4). But God promised something more than comfort. And God has delivered something more than comfort. In Jesus we are awaiting a *joy to come* that we can barely conceive of now. The *risen* Lord Jesus is the reason why those who weep are told they are "blessed", since they "shall laugh" (Luke 6 v 21).

Laughter is a loaded word in the Bible. Abraham's wife, Sarah, laughed when she heard God promise her husband that they would have a son—they were both very old, and she had been unable to have children (Genesis 18 v 10-12). That was the laughter of ridicule: "yeah, right". Perhaps you sometimes feel that way when you read about the resurrection: yeah, right. The gospel is promising something so good we dare not believe it for self-protective reasons. Remember Thomas? We are hurting badly enough already, we don't want to be let down by anything more. But God tells the truth.

Abraham and Sarah did indeed have a baby boy, and he

was named Isaac, which means "laughter" (Genesis 21 v 1-3). Sarah's laughter of ridicule gave way to the joyous, astonished laughter of a delighted mother. God kept his outrageous promise. We too can believe that a day truly is coming when, through Jesus, our age of tears will break into an age of shouts of joy. When mealtimes of emptiness, fear, and loss give way to mealtimes of feasting and wholeness. Maybe we cannot conceive of how, but we do know that it *will*.

The central joy of the life to come is that we will dwell face to face with our dear Lord Jesus. To know the Father through him for ever, no longer hindered by our own sin and the brokenness of this present but passing age. Because of this central joy, all the other joys will be all the more lovely. To enjoy life—normal, human life—in right relationship with God and one another. To work, to play, to eat, to rest, to sing, to create, to talk, to laugh, to love. To know a level of intimacy in human relations that we only ever glimpse at best in this life. To keep going deeper, and deeper, and deeper, with no end in sight. Always under the warm, steady, sure and tender gaze of Jesus our Lord.

Our *dear Lord Jesus* who, we know, is near to the broken-hearted.

> *So we do not lose heart. Though our outer self is wasting away, our inner self is being renewed day by day. For this light momentary affliction is preparing for us an eternal weight of glory beyond all comparison, as we look not to the things that are seen but to the things that are unseen. For the things that are seen are transient, but the things that are unseen are eternal. (2 Corinthians 4 v 16-18)*

> *Amen. Come, Lord Jesus! (Revelation 22 v 20)*

Appendix I

Further practical advice for grief

In the following pages, you can find more details on a number of practical ideas for coping with grief.

LAMENT

We mentioned the Bible's laments in chapters 1 and 4. Here are some steps we can take as we trace the Bible's laments and make them our own.

- Start by reading part or all of Psalm 13, 22, 88 or 102. Other psalms of lament are 3, 5, 6, 7, 17, 25, 26, 27, 28, 38, 39, 42, 43, 44, 51, 54, 55, 56, 57, 59, 61, 63, 64, 69, 70, 71, 74, 79, 80, 83, 86, 89, 109, 120, 130.
- You might find it helpful to copy out a few verses, or the whole thing, making the words your own.
- You might also find it helpful to use particular verses as a starting point for writing about your own experience of the same thing. For example, you may feel familiar with the feeling expressed in Psalm 13 v 1: "How long O Lord? Will you forget me for ever? How long will you hide your face from me?" Based on this, you could write a few lines of personal

lament: "I don't see how I can keep going like this, Father. Every day I wake up feeling numb and nothing is comforting me." As we "trace" the Bible's laments in this way, we not only find nooks and crannies within which our own grief is expressed, but we are also gently helped to trace out faith in the Lord in dark times. So when we get to Psalm 13 v 5 for instance, which says, "But I have trusted in your steadfast love; my heart shall rejoice in your salvation", we might one day be able to write, "Please help me to keep trusting in you, Father. I know that you are good all the time."

- Keep going. A verse or two a day might seem like nothing, but through the hard and slow months they will compound into shaping the way you think and feel towards God. And there'll be surprising times along the way where words may pour out of you.

MINI-JOURNALLING

The time to start talking about your grief is not later, it's now. Start talking honestly with others if you haven't already. Maybe you have no difficulty expressing honestly what you feel. But for many people, the practice of honest expression is hard: you are not used to telling others how you feel or even acknowledging it to yourself.

Here's a suggestion: start by keeping a private journal. It doesn't have to be long—just a single line each day, maybe— but it will help your self-awareness and thus help you to relate better to others. You could start with the following questions:

- *What am I feeling and why?* This question helps to build our own internal self-awareness. If you find it hard to name how you are feeling, you could look up a "feelings wheel" on the internet and get into the habit of using it to locate the feeling which best describes you in a given moment. Asking "why" helps to get beneath the surface of an emotion and builds a greater degree of emotional fluency.

• *How does God feel about me and why?* This question reframes our feelings within a bigger reality; it gets us to feel in light of the gospel. The answer to this question is that, if I am trusting in Jesus, God is delighted in me as his child. I am a treasure and a pleasure to him—because I am in Jesus. I need to keep remembering this because my heart is constantly prone to redefine what God is like.

Alternatively, ask, *What is today's "but" and why?* Look back at the postscript to chapter 1 to see how the word "but" redirects our attention. Write your own three-step thought process each day.

Once you're used to doing that, start to share honestly with someone you trust. With grief, there are no experts: we are all muddling through, taking baby steps together. If you are a couple, it may be that you're each handling this quite differently, and that's very normal; it's ok. For perhaps most couples, navigating this difference of communication and expression will be one of the challenges you'll need to recognise and accept together.

BUDGETING ATTENTION

Processing grief has a way of slowing you down—drastically. Thoughts, decisions, ideas, conversations and emotions become hard work. Have you ever tried to use a really slow laptop? You try to do something really simple—like open a webpage—and it takes *ages*. You wonder what on earth it's doing. Usually it's because the processes your laptop is running in the background are using up a huge proportion of the computer's memory (RAM)—and there's no way to close it down. This is what grief is like. Because grief is so consuming, and can't be simply shut down, everything else gets drastically slowed.

Do you relate to this? Again and again we've felt like slow laptops running a big programme in the background. Simple decisions took us ages to make; we were constantly exhausted.

What we need to do in this situation is make a kind of budget for what we're going to pay attention to.

First, try to make a list of the separate stressors in your life. To return to the computer analogy, what are the processes running in your mind? It doesn't really matter about the order, just try to get things out of your head. E.g.:

1. *Not sleeping well.*
2. *Need to make shopping list and plan what we'll eat next week.*
3. *Car service is due.*
4. *Dreading conversations with XYZ.*

Second, next to each item, write down what you (or others) could do to help ease or resolve that thought or stressor. Even if there's something which would only make a 1% difference, write it down. If ten things can be eased by 1% each, that's a much easier mind. The point here is, even if I can't fix the grief in the centre of my life right now, I can take tiny steps to ease the pain of its ripples.

1. *Not sleeping well. Keep notepad and Bible next to bed, write down everything on my mind as I go to bed? Read*

Psalm 23 or 46 before I fall asleep? Don't drink caffeine
after 3pm?
2. *Need to make shopping list and plan what we'll eat next
week. Buy big bags of frozen food and frozen vegetables,
then we'll always have some back ups? Ask Jim (leader
from church) if he could ask people to provide a few
meals each week?*
3. *Car service due. Ask my brother to book it and make
any decisions about repairs, he likes cars?*
4. *Dreading conversations with XYZ. Message Tim and
Sarah from church and ask them to pray about it?*

Third, decide which of these steps you can action straight
away. It's about closing down all the "open loops" that you
possibly can. So start with the things which will disappear
from your list as soon as they're done. Once a loop is fully
closed it can't cause you any additional stress. Free up as much
margin as you can. If you are a friend or family member,
do whatever you can to help with this. Don't say, "If there's
anything I can do to help, please do give me a call". This
actually opens a new loop: now they have to think, decide,
and get back to you about how you could help. Instead,
present a simple yes or no question: "Would you like us to
drop round some freezer meals tonight after 6pm?"

Finally, make a plan for when you are going to pay attention
to the other items on the list. For example, if the car service is
on your mind but it isn't actually due for three weeks, make
a note to think about it in ten days' time. You haven't closed
the loop, but this might help you to stop paying attention to
it when you don't need to.

THOUGHT PLAYLISTS

The great thing about a playlist is that once someone's made it, all you have to do is click play and let it run. A thought playlist is simply a sequence of thoughts which you've put together in advance. It's another easy way of stewarding and directing our attention as we grieve and as our minds are maxed out.

- It might be an actual music playlist of songs and hymns that help you to hear wonderful gospel truths. We started one in the first few weeks after learning about Jed's health problems. At the time he was just known as "twin 2". And so, to this day we have a Spotify playlist called "Anna's twin 2 songs". Whenever we came across a hymn or song that helped us rehearse glorious gospel truth, we added it to the playlist. Whenever we were struggling we would put it on. We often still put it on.

- It might consist of bits of writing. Maybe a handful of Bible verses which you keep on your phone; or a prayer which you can read at times when you can't string two words together. The wisdom of this is that you have something ready to grab at a moment's notice. If you find yourself overwhelmed with panic, anger or sadness while you are in the grocery aisle or in the car park or wherever, you can look at your thought playlist and use it to help you pray.

- It can be helpful to choose in advance particular songs, Bible verses or prayers for particular emotions. For example, "When I feel dread, I will read Psalm 27". Or, "When I feel empty, I will read Psalm 23". The point is that you've made the decision ahead of time so that when you realise you're in the midst of deep dark emotions, you aren't left panicking about what to do.

EARLY WARNING SCORES

An Early Warning Score is used in healthcare to try to spot when a seemingly stable patient might be about to deteriorate. The healthcare professional logs a few simple measurements and adds up the score. In our version, you ask yourself a few easy questions each day, and share the score with someone you trust. For instance, each day you might count the following:

- How many hours sleep fewer than eight did I get?
- How many cups of coffee did I drink today?
- How many times have I snapped at the children, multiplied by 3?
- How many units of alcohol have I consumed today?

You could ask your friend to help you come up with a list that is relevant to you. Together you might decide a certain number which, if you score it, indicates that something needs to change. Alternatively, you might just use it to help you notice trends: what's normal and stable, and what's a slight dip. In grief, you may have a good patch, but then something might knock you into a downward spiral. We all want to spot that spiral as early as possible.

EXTRA NOTES ON MARRIAGE AND FAMILY
Patterns of communication:
If in doubt, communicate more, not less. The communication doesn't have to be pretty or coherent. Our co-author, Chris, recommends constant "normalisation":

"We normalized with each other by constantly verbalizing where we were in the grief process. If one of us was hit with a wave of grief and the tears began to flow, the other would 'check in' and the griever would verbalize exactly how they felt and what caused the tears. Even though we had different triggers and different minor crises of faith, we learned to appreciate each other's grief. So, I recommend constant normalization and verbalization during the first year and a half or so, or whatever is appropriate for you."

Carve out and protect time simply to be together, even if you're silent. It might be a time when you both write or journal, or when you go and walk in the park together. Just because you may be feeling and processing grief differently on any given day doesn't mean that you can't do this journey in relationship to one another. You can always say a prayer, even a short one, together. "Father, please help us to keep trusting you. Help us to get through this. Please give us strength enough for this day."

The more routines you can make automatic—a "default setting"—the more headspace you will have and the less strain you will feel. Think about your calendar default settings. Perhaps Monday afternoons could be when you take time as a couple; Tuesday evenings when your parents come round for a meal; Wednesday when you see friends from church regularly; Thursday the day you keep ruthlessly clear; Friday when you get a treat supper with the children and watch a movie; and so on. Think about your conversational default settings: what are going to be the things you say routinely? The questions you ask your spouse and children? The verses and hymns which come to mind?

If you have other children, encourage communication as best you can. Encourage them to express how they are feeling, and to make the child you have lost a normal part of conversation. Revisit photos and other memories of their life often. Encourage questions, and don't fear the questions which you find hard. Model to your children how you are struggling towards the Lord.

Setting expectations:
It's well worth having an honest think about your expectations, and being willing to have those challenged. How long do you think it will take to "get over this"? Can you accept that you will never get over this fully? When you feel tired and underslept, you will probably always start to feel sad about the one you have lost. What about your expectations of one another? Can you accept that you and your spouse will likely not be in perfect sync in your journey through this? That one of you will likely take far longer to get back to any degree of normal functioning? Be prepared to be patient with each other when you are out of sync.

Seeking support:
Every marriage and family needs support from others. The path of wisdom lies in nurturing deep and trusting relationships outside of your nuclear family. If possible, involve grandparents in weekly rhythms that become defaults. Perhaps there is a friend or relative who could have the children for dinner one evening a week.

A guiding principle is, no matter how extroverted you are, go deep with a few, and be wise with the many. You simply can't walk closely with everyone. Be ready to share honestly in a succinct way with everyone who asks, and committed to sharing deeply with a few close brothers and sisters in Christ.

Appendix II

Further reading and resources

On the Bible's laments:

- *Dark Clouds, Deep Mercy: Discovering the Grace of Lament* by Mark Vroegop

For help to explain what the Bible has to say about suffering:

- *How Long, O Lord? Reflections on Suffering and Evil* by D.A. Carson
- *Walking with God through Pain and Suffering* by Timothy Keller

For those in a deep and dark valley:

- *Depression: Looking up from the Stubborn Darkness* by Edward Welch
- *When I Don't Desire God* by John Piper

For those wanting to explore further whether Jesus' resurrection really happened:

- *The Son Rises: Historical Evidence for the Resurrection of Jesus* by William Lane Craig
- *The Case for Easter* by Lee Strobel

On how we can be sure that God does not punish Jesus' followers for their sin:

- *Is Forgiveness Really Free?* by Michael Jensen
- *How Can I Be Sure?* by John Stevens

For young children who are losing a sibling:

- *The Moon is Always Round* by Jonathan Gibson and Joe Hox

On parenting, when the challenges you face are not what you would have expected or asked for:

- *The Life You Never Expected: Parenting Special Needs Children* by Andrew and Rachel Wilson

On what happens to young children after they die:

- *Safe in the Arms of God: Truth from Heaven about the Death of a Child* by John MacArthur

On the value of human life:

- *Matters of Life and Death* by John Wyatt

Three Christian classics which have provided comfort for broken-hearted Christians down through the ages:

- *A Divine Cordial (All Things for Good)* by Thomas Watson
- *The Bruised Reed* by Richard Sibbes
- *The Letters of Samuel Rutherford* by Samuel Rutherford

Organisations that can help:

- In the UK, Winston's Wish (www.winstonswish. org) is a charitable organisation that exists to help children and young people navigate grief.
- There are likely to be bereavement services linked to your local hospital; these may offer counselling for grieving parents and families.
- Crisis pregnancy centres exist around the world to support women who are pregnant and need support. You can find if there is one near you by searching "crisis pregnancy centre". In the UK, you can call the pregnancy crisis helpline for free, confidential support (0800 368 9296, www. pregnancycrisishelpline.org.uk).

Above all, please do connect with a good church, if you are not already part of one. This is because a good church will make God known as he really is—in the Jesus of the Bible. And as we keep knowing Jesus, we will be strengthened and comforted. There is no perfect church, but there really is no greater comfort than the biblical gospel which faithful churches proclaim.

Acknowledgements

DAN AND ANNA:
This book would not exist were it not for the kindness and support shown to us by our church family, Grace Church Gateshead. Thank you for being family to us in Jesus through the pregnancy, and then through Jed's life and death and the aftermath. Thank you for enabling a sabbatical a few years later, during which we were able to turn our various notes into this little book. We love you and are indebted to you. Any royalties from this book are being paid directly to Grace Church, since these pages represent an indirect ministry of the church.

We thank our biological families, in particular both our sets of parents, for their incredible and steadfast support. To our children, Lois, Esther and Ethan: thank you for being such joys, for being examples to us of how to trust God, and for lifting our spirits.

To our dear friends, along with church and family: we can't put into words our gratitude to you and our love for you. You truly have been examples of how to "walk alongside" those who suffer. We thank God for the precious, deepened relationships that we enjoy with you through your willingness to journey with us.

We sincerely thank the staff of the Neonatal Intensive Care Unit at the Royal Victoria Infirmary, Newcastle-upon-Tyne, for their excellent care.

We vigorously thank and applaud Katy Morgan and her colleagues at The Good Book Company for their diligent, gracious and masterful guidance throughout the process of bringing this book into existence. And to Chris Mouring: thank you for your willingness to share your story here, and for your encouragements at every stage. This whole book, not just your chapter, has been vastly enriched by your wisdom and insight.

Finally, this book exists because there is some*one* worth writing about. Above all we thank you, Lord Jesus, for comforting us, strengthening us, loving us, leading us. We are yours! Every page here boasts of your nearness to the broken-hearted.

CHRIS:
Writing brings such clarity to a story. The participants in the story and those involved in its retelling are brought to the forefront of the writer's heart and mind. Even now, tears of gratitude and wonder flow as I think again of the many, many people that have been near to us in our broken-hearted but hope-filled journey. Most cannot be named; all are loved and appreciated.

To my wife, Kim: thank you for your incredible strength, persistent love, and spiritual insight. Even though you have endured so much devastation, you have been a rock that points me to *the* Rock, Jesus. I may have put pen to paper, but this is *our* story. Thank you for continuing to be a valuable and an inseparable part of it.

To our children, Rachel, Matthew, Philip, and goddaughter Lindsay: thank you for how you continue to enrich our family in our shared path of grief even as you have each personally shouldered so much.

To Dan and Anna Martin: thank you for the privilege of being a small part of this book and for blessing me with your sharp spiritual insight and warm encouragement. You are a great example of connecting truth with life in love. The providential collision of our two grief journeys has made our own journey a little easier, a little richer.

To Katy Morgan of The Good Book Company: thank you for your editorial and spiritual insights that have amazed and blessed me. I have learned much in the distilling of our story under your care.

Most importantly, thank you, Lord Jesus, for being near to us, for sustaining us, for making us more than conquerors by your love in the midst of very dark providences. In our broken-heartedness, we have good and great hope only because of you.

thegoodbook
COMPANY

BIBLICAL | RELEVANT | ACCESSIBLE

At The Good Book Company, we are dedicated to helping Christians and local churches grow. We believe that God's growth process always starts with hearing clearly what he has said to us through his timeless word—the Bible.

Ever since we opened our doors in 1991, we have been striving to produce Bible-based resources that bring glory to God. We have grown to become an international provider of user-friendly resources to the Christian community, with believers of all backgrounds and denominations using our books, Bible studies, devotionals, evangelistic resources, and DVD-based courses.

We want to equip ordinary Christians to live for Christ day by day, and churches to grow in their knowledge of God, their love for one another, and the effectiveness of their outreach.

Call us for a discussion of your needs or visit one of our local websites for more information on the resources and services we provide.

Your friends at The Good Book Company

thegoodbook.com | thegoodbook.co.uk
thegoodbook.com.au | thegoodbook.co.nz
thegoodbook.co.in